CHOSEN LIFELINES 365

An Artful Guide for Daily Living

Charmaine Jennings
Walter Jennings

Tampa, FL

Copyright © 2023 by Charmaine Jennings, Walter Jennings

All rights reserved. This book is protected by the copyright laws of the United States of America. This book may not be copied or reprinted for commercial gain or profit. No copies of this book or any parts of this book can be reprinted or disseminated in any form including- electronic, mechanical, photocopy, recording, or otherwise unless you have prior written permission from the publisher.

Chosen Lifelines 365
by Charmaine Jennings, Walter Jennings
Rain Publishing
info@rainpublishing.com
www.rainpublishing.com

Front and Back Cover Designs by Charmaine & Walter Jennings

Unless otherwise noted, all scriptures are taken from the English Standard Version Bible.

Chosen Lifelines 365/Charmaine Jennings, Walter Jennings – 1st edition

ISBN: 978-0-9977748-9-4

DEDICATION

This 365 day artful guide for living is dedicated to the individual committed to personal growth and development. May your relationship with yourself become stronger and healthier. May your relationships with family members, friends, co-workers and the extended community flourish as a result of your personal journey. May you engage in the artful challenges and introspection that will lead to a mental and physical metamorphosis.
Enjoy and share your experience with us.

365 DAY GUIDE

CONTENTS

- **12 Key Principles:** Introductions
- **12 Key Principle Affirmations:** Individuals
- **12 Key Principle Affirmations:** Couples, Family, Friends, and Community Groups
- **84 Art Challenges: 7 per Month:** Before Day 1, After Day 7, 15 & 23
- **365 Days of Reflection & Introspection**

  Featuring:

  365 Thoughtful Quotes

  365+ Compelling Questions

  365 Bible Scriptures

  365 Journal Entry Spaces

- **1 Coloring Book:** Each page in your 365 day artful guide will beg you to add color!

  #GoForIt #AddValue #MakeYourMark

- **Meet The Authors:** Charmaine & Walter Jennings

"If you do the work, it will show."
"If you don't do the work, it will show."
~Walter Jennings

PREFACE

"Watch your thoughts, they become your words; watch your words, they become your actions; watch your actions, they become your habits; watch your habits, they become your character; watch your character, it becomes your destiny." –Lao Tzu

The average person thinks more than 50,000 thoughts per day. More than half of those thoughts are negative and more than 90% are just repeats from the day before (Wood, 2013). Researchers have proven that self-reflection time must be intentional in order to be effective. This allows people to refocus the mind on the positive.

What is it about us that fixates on the negative more than the positive? Limited positive introspection time leads to limited growth and development. Introspection is an important psychological exercise that can help us grow, develop our minds and extract value from our mistakes. The reflection process is to examine one's own internal thoughts and feelings in order to determine what they mean. The process can be focused on either one's current mental experience or experiences from the past.

Enhancing our ability to understand ourselves, our motivations, and to learn more about our own values is priceless. We can take the power away from the distractions of our modern, fast-paced lives to refocus on fulfillment (Wood, 2013).

As you engage with this 365-day artful guide, be mindful that a healthy balance of introspection is encouraged. Reflection time that leads to obsessive thoughts and behaviors, may result in less than positive results (Eurich, 2017).

Are you ready to enhance self-expression, self-awareness, diverse learning modalities and personal development? Are you ready to add value to your communication styles and interactions with other people? Chosen Life Specialists, LLC excels in combining introspection and arts-infused coaching techniques and strategies that include but are not limited to: acting, dance and movement, body awareness, music, drawing, painting, fashion, culinary, crafts, etc. Our arts-infused coaching and counseling methods support personal growth and development, thus strengthening various areas of wellness and well-being.

This 365-day artful guide to daily living seeks to captivate the soul, body and mind in ways that verbal expression alone may limit. This experience will provoke you to think, create, and act. This art-infused approach supports emotional, spiritual and social well-being, healing, and recovery through a person-centered approach.

Walter & Charmaine Jennings

CHOSEN LIFE

is an acronym and philosophy that represents 12 key principles:

C.H.O.S.E.N.

You are **called** to evolve and succeed above and beyond anything you can imagine. You see **challenges** as temporary distractions that attempt to prevent goals and dreams from being achieved. You embrace **change** as a necessary ingredient for success and significance. You are **heart-healthy, open-minded** and willing to **sacrifice** and **surrender**. You know that **everywhere matters** and wisdom **never says never**.

L.I.F.E.

You invest in **living not existing**, focus on the **inside out before the outside in** and you are **fearless not fearful** because **every day counts**.

Motto

"Called to Challenge and Change Relationship Culture."

—Walter & Charmaine Jennings

Scripture

"For many are called, but few are chosen."

-Matthew 22:14

ME?! AM I CALLED?

CALLED

Is there anything more distinct (and sometimes disturbing) as hearing your parent call your name? You may attempt to ignore it, but even when you don't respond...you can FEEL it. You roll your eyes. The hairs on your arm stand at attention. Your throat tightens. Eventually, the gears in your mind start turning: "What do they want NOW?!" "Am I in trouble?" "Maybe they will go away if I don't say anything."

The problem is that even if you don't answer, you KNOW you were called. Can you deny their appeal without denying yourself? What happens when life starts calling? It is possible that in our effort to block out the demands of people and problems fighting for our attention, we may be inadvertently abandoning the opportunities we say we want for ourselves. If "call" means to 'cry out', what potential tears and traumas are we ignoring that we're possibly equipped to address?

The potential solution may seem obvious, but still can be difficult to initiate. Answer the call. This doesn't mean that you're signing up to be the superhero to save the day. It doesn't mean you have all the answers. It definitely doesn't mean that the magnitude of the situation rests completely on your shoulders. However, this simple acknowledgment opens the door for you to become a part of the solution. It means that you've recognized the call and made yourself available to hear its demands. You were called for a reason. Will you answer?

CALLED: AFFIRMATION

ME, MYSELF & I

I am destined to remain kind to myself, to date myself forever and to build a life that reflects purpose, passion and personal growth. I will evolve in selfless love, forgiveness, and trust. I am committed to growing, remaining focused and intentional.

WE

We are destined to remain friends, to invest quality time, and to build a life together through marriage, family, friendship, and community relationships. We will learn selfless love, forgiveness, trust, and partnership. We are committed to growing, thus remaining focused and purposeful in our union.

ART CHALLENGE #1

VISUAL ART

Utilize photography, painting, digital media, sketching, sculpture, collage, crafts, etc. to represent the Chosen Life principle through visual art.

CHALLENGE

Create a visual that represents you succeeding in your life's purpose work.

JANUARY 1

CALLED

"Some are born great, some achieve greatness, and some have greatness thrust upon them." –William Shakespeare

What type of work(s) are you compelled to do when no one is watching or waiting to give praise and acknowledgement? Why?

_____
_____
_____
_____
_____
_____
_____
_____
_____
_____

Romans 1:1,6-7 "Paul, a servant of Christ Jesus, called to be an apostle and set apart for the gospel of God. And you also are among those Gentiles who are called to belong to Jesus Christ. To all in Rome who are loved by God and called to be his holy people: Grace and peace to you from God our Father and from the Lord Jesus Christ." ESV

JANUARY 2

CALLED

"I believe every one of us is born with a purpose. No matter who you are, what you do, or how far you think you have to go, you have been tapped by a force greater than yourself to step into your God-given calling." ~Oprah Winfrey

Who or what fuels the work(s) that you are compelled to do when no one is watching or waiting to give praise and acknowledgement? Why?

_____
_____
_____
_____
_____
_____
_____
_____
_____
_____

Romans 10:12-13 "For there is no difference between Jew and Gentile—the same Lord is Lord of all and richly blesses all who call on him, for, Everyone who calls on the name of the Lord will be saved." ESV

JANUARY 3

CALLED

"When God calls us to a task, He will equip us. God doesn't call the qualified, He qualifies the called." ~Anonymous

What are you called to do to encourage, help or enhance situations or other people? How do you know you were called to these things?

_____
_____
_____
_____
_____
_____
_____
_____
_____
_____
_____
_____

Revelation 17:14 "They will wage war against the Lamb, but the Lamb will triumph over them because he is Lord of lords and King of kings—and with him will be his called, chosen and faithful followers." ESV

JANUARY 4

CALLED

"Catharsis returns us to the purpose for which were originally intended – to be called by God to do good – and thus ultimately returns us to our authentic selves." ~Desmond Tutu

Who are you called to become in order to encourage, help or enhance situations or other people? Would you make any character enhancements? Why?

_____

_____

_____

_____

_____

_____

_____

_____

_____

_____

_____

2 Thessalonians 2:14 "He called you to this through our gospel, that you might share in the glory of our Lord Jesus Christ." ESV

JANUARY 5

CALLED

"Calling is not only a matter of being and doing what we ARE, but also evolving into what we are not YET called by God to become and do." ~Os Guinness

Who do you predict you will become in 5-10 years as your calling continues to be revealed and you answer? Why?

_____
_____
_____
_____
_____
_____
_____
_____
_____
_____
_____
_____
_____

2 Peter 1:10 "Give diligence to make your calling and election sure." ESV

JANUARY 6

CALLED

"God is calling you, equipping you, preparing you according to His purpose. If God called you to a task, He will then qualify you for the job." ~Anonymous

Are you being called to follow and/or to lead? Why or why not?
Who are you currently following and/or leading? Is it helping or harming?

_____
_____
_____
_____
_____
_____
_____
_____

Joel 2:28-32 "And afterward, I will pour out my Spirit on all people. Your sons and daughters will prophesy, your old men will dream dreams, your young men will see visions. Even on my servants, both men and women, I will pour out my Spirit in those days. I will show wonders in the heavens and on the earth, blood and fire and billows of smoke. The sun will be turned to darkness and the moon to blood before the coming of the great and dreadful day of the Lord. And everyone who calls on the name of the Lord will be saved; for on Mount Zion and in Jerusalem there will be deliverance, as the Lord has said, even among the survivors whom the Lord calls." ESV

JANUARY 7

CALLED

"Since God alone provides the means for the successful accomplishment of any task, it seems evident that a person needs to be called by God to be an effective teacher. Without this call to teaching, how will anyone be able to put up with everything that teachers face daily?" ~Basil Moreau

What and who have you been called to teach in the past? Present? What have you learned about yourself? What have you learned about your teaching style?

_____
_____
_____
_____
_____
_____
_____
_____

Acts 10:31-33 "'Cornelius, God has heard your prayer and remembered your gifts to the poor. Send to Joppa for Simon who is called Peter. He is a guest in the home of Simon the tanner, who lives by the sea.' So I sent for you immediately, and it was good of you to come. Now we are all here in the presence of God to listen to everything the Lord has commanded you to tell us." ESV

ART CHALLENGE #2

WORD ART

Utilize acrostic poetry, short stories, word cloud, etc. to represent the Chosen Life principle through word art.

CHALLENGE

Design word art using 5 power words that represent you succeeding in your purpose work.

ART CHALLENGE #3

MOVEMENT ART

Utilize dance, human twister poses, acting, etc. to represent the Chosen Life principle through movement art.

CHALLENGE

Create a pose (i.e. movement art) that represents the day you discover(ed) your passion work.

JANUARY 8

CALLED

"Don't chase your call. Chase the God who calls you. Call on the name of the Lord and be saved." ~Anonymous

How do you know for certain that you are being called?
How do you distinguish between your own wants and desires and God's?

_____
_____
_____
_____
_____
_____
_____
_____
_____
_____
_____
_____

Matthew 6:33-34 "But seek first His kingdom and His righteousness, and all these things will be given to you as well. Therefore do not worry about tomorrow, for tomorrow will worry about itself. Each day has enough trouble of its own." ESV

JANUARY 9

CALLED

"God's calling requires action. When God calls you, he calls collect...you better be willing to accept the charges of your calling." ~Steve Maraboli

What and how much has your calling cost you?
Is it worth the costly charges? Why or why not?

___

Mark 16:15 "He said to them, "Go into all the world and preach the gospel to all creation." ESV

JANUARY 10

CALLED

"Since God alone provides the means for the successful accomplishment of any task, it seems evident that a person needs to be called by God to be an effective teacher. Without this call to teaching, how will anyone be able to put up with everything that teachers face daily?" ~Basil Moreau

Got stamina? Got muscles? How has your calling required you to exercise a deeper level of patience, peace and long-term dedication to the assigned work(s)?

_____
_____
_____
_____
_____
_____
_____
_____

1 Corinthians 7:17 "Nevertheless, each person should live as a believer in whatever situation the Lord has assigned to them, just as God has called them. This is the rule I lay down in all the churches." ESV

JANUARY 11

CALLED

"God calls you priceless, beloved, and friend, so don't lose any sleep over what anybody else calls you!" –Anonymous

How do you respond to rejection or name-calling? Who has the loudest voice in your life? Why? Which voices add value? How?

_____
_____
_____
_____
_____
_____
_____
_____
_____

Ephesians 4:1-6 "As a prisoner for the Lord, then, I urge you to live a life worthy of the calling you have received. Be completely humble and gentle; be patient, bearing with one another in love. Make every effort to keep the unity of the Spirit through the bond of peace. There is one body and one Spirit, just as you were called to one hope when you were called; one Lord, one faith, one baptism; One God and Father of all, who is over all and through all and in all." ESV

JANUARY 12

CALLED

"Your life is too valuable, your calling too great and your God too awesome to waste your life on what doesn't matter." ~Anonymous

How is your calling making a difference in the lives of others?
Who are these people? What has been the impact?

_____
_____
_____
_____
_____
_____
_____
_____
_____

Philippians 2:1-4 "Therefore if you have any encouragement from being united with Christ, if any comfort from his love, if any common sharing in the Spirit, if any tenderness and compassion, then make my joy complete by being like-minded, having the same love, being one in spirit and of one mind. Do nothing out of selfish ambition or vain conceit. Rather, in humility value others above yourselves, not looking to your own interests but each of you to the interests of the others." ESV

JANUARY 13

CALLED

"When God calls us to step out of our comfort zone, He is not calling us to be comfortable in the situation. He is calling us to be comfortable in Him in spite of the situation." -Anonymous

How has your calling caused you to step outside of your comfort zone? What does this look, feel, and sound like? What has been the positive impact?

_____
_____
_____
_____
_____
_____
_____
_____
_____

Philippians 3:12-14 "Not that I have already obtained all this or have already arrived at my goal, but I press on to take hold of that for which Christ Jesus took hold of me. Brothers and sisters, I do not consider myself yet to have taken hold of it. But one thing I do: Forgetting what is behind and straining toward what is ahead, I press on toward the goal to win the prize for which God has called me heavenward in Christ Jesus." ESV

JANUARY 14

CALLED

"When you have been called by God, you must live a life worthy of the calling." ~Anonymous

Does your lifestyle match the requirements of the calling? How?
Do you worry about hypocrisy? Why or why not?

_____
_____
_____
_____
_____
_____
_____
_____
_____
_____

2 Timothy 1:10 "But it has now been revealed through the appearing of our Savior, Christ Jesus, who has destroyed death and has brought life and immortality to light through the gospel." ESV

JANUARY 15

CALLED

"When God calls you to something, He is not calling you to succeed, He's calling you to obey! The success of the calling is up to God; the obedience is up to you." –Anonymous

How well do you obey? Describe a time when you obeyed and the outcome was amazing. Mention a time when you didn't obey and things didn't end well.

_____
_____
_____
_____
_____
_____
_____
_____
_____
_____
_____

Hebrews 3:1 "Therefore, holy brothers and sisters, who share in the heavenly calling, fix your thoughts on Jesus, whom we acknowledge as our apostle and high priest." ESV

ART CHALLENGE #4

MUSIC ART

Utilize instrumentals, lyrics, or diverse genres to represent the Chosen Life principle through music art.

CHALLENGE

Find a special song that represents saying "yes" to a new opportunity.

ART CHALLENGE #5

CULINARY ART

Utilize cooking, baking, drink design, and the 5 senses (sight, touch, smell, taste, and hearing) to represent the Chosen Life principle through culinary art.

CHALLENGE

Find a fragrance/scent that reminds you of a new beginning or direction.

JANUARY 16

CALLED

"God often uses our pain as a launching pad of our greatest calling." ~Anonymous

How have you utilized the pain and/or hurt in your life to enhance, help or encourage other people or situations? What was the outcome?

_____
_____
_____
_____
_____
_____
_____
_____
_____
_____
_____

Romans 8:18 "For I consider that the sufferings of this present time are not worth comparing with the glory that is to be revealed to us." ESV

JANUARY 17

CALLED

"God's calling is according to His predestination, His purpose, and His grace." ~Anonymous

How has the plan and purpose (i.e. destiny) for your life been slowly revealed throughout your lifespan? Is there an obvious pattern?

_____
_____
_____
_____
_____
_____
_____
_____
_____
_____
_____
_____

Psalms 139:13-14 "For you created my inmost being; you knit me together in my mother's womb. I praise you because I am fearfully and wonderfully made; your works are wonderful, I know that full well." ESV

JANUARY 18

CALLED

"God did not direct His call to Isaiah— Isaiah overheard God saying, ". . . who will go for Us?" The call of God is not just for a select few but for everyone. Whether I hear God's call or not depends on the condition of my ears, and exactly what I hear depends upon my spiritual attitude." — Oswald Chambers

What is the condition of your ears and spiritual attitude? Is it helping or hurting? Building Up or Breaking Down? Why or why not?

_____
_____
_____
_____
_____
_____
_____
_____
_____

Proverbs 15:31 "The ear that listens to life-giving reproof will dwell among the wise." ESV

JANUARY 19

CALLED

"Raising your children to love and serve Jesus is fulfilling one of God's highest callings upon your life." — Elizabeth George

How is your calling impacting the young minds of today? How will you allow your calling to be contagious? Will you use it to support future generations?

_____
_____
_____
_____
_____
_____
_____
_____
_____
_____

Mark 10:13-16 "And they were bringing children to him that he might touch them, and the disciples rebuked them. But when Jesus saw it, he was indignant and said to them, "Let the children come to me; do not hinder them, for to such belongs the kingdom of God. Truly, I say to you, whoever does not receive the kingdom of God like a child shall not enter it." And he took them in his arms and blessed them, laying his hands on them." ESV

JANUARY 20

CALLED

"A job is a vocation only if someone else calls you to do it for them rather than for yourself. And so our work can be a calling only if it is reimagined as a mission of service to something beyond merely our own interests. Thinking of work mainly as a means of self-fulfillment and self-realization slowly crushes a person."
— Timothy Keller

How are you serving something beyond your own interests? Is it self-fulfillment and self-realization is the unexpected reward for obeying the call? Why or why not?

_____
_____
_____
_____
_____
_____
_____

Colossians 3:17 "And whatever you do, in word or deed, do everything in the name of the Lord Jesus, giving thanks to God the Father through him." ESV

JANUARY 21

CALLED

"Don't let someone keep putting out the flame God keeps relighting, we all have a purpose. As a wing to a bird. As wind that goes the destiny over the sea." — Anthony Liccione

How does the light of your unique calling remain lit and shine bright when faced with criticism or conflict?

_____
_____
_____
_____
_____
_____
_____
_____
_____
_____
_____
_____

Matthew 5:16 "In the same way, let your light shine before others, so that they may see your good works and give glory to your Father who is in heaven." ESV

JANUARY 22

CALLED

"Everybody has a vocation to some form of life-work. However, behind that call (and deeper than any call), everybody has a vocation to be a person to be fully and deeply human in Christ Jesus." — Brennan Manning

What would you do if your current work (i.e. career, job) does not align with your passion? What would you do if your work conflicts with your personal values and principles?

_____
_____
_____
_____
_____
_____
_____
_____
_____

Joshua 24:15 "And if it is evil in your eyes to serve the Lord, choose this day whom you will serve, whether the gods your fathers served in the region beyond the River, or the gods of the Amorites in whose land you dwell. But as for me and my house, we will serve the Lord." ESV

JANUARY 23

CALLED

"We are never short on opportunities to answer the call to assist the widows, support the homeless, stand up for justice and to preach Christ crucified and resurrected. That is the true calling of every believer." — Andrena Sawyer

How has "the calling" and unique opportunities required you to support the widow, assist the homeless, and stand up for justice? What was/is the impact? Does/did it lead people toward a better life (i.e. purpose, salvation, joy)?

_____
_____
_____
_____
_____
_____

Matthew 25:35-40 "For I was hungry and you gave me food, I was thirsty and you gave me drink, I was a stranger and you welcomed me, I was naked and you clothed me, I was sick and you visited me, I was in prison and you came to me.' Then the righteous will answer him, saying, 'Lord, when did we see you hungry and feed you, or thirsty and give you drink? And when did we see you a stranger and welcome you, or naked and clothe you? And when did we see you sick or in prison and visit you?' And the King will answer them, 'Truly, I say to you, as you did it to one of the least of these my brothers, you did it to me." ESV

ART CHALLENGE #6

FASHION ART

Utilize clothing, make-up, or jewelry art, interior design work, etc. to represent the Chosen Life principle through fashion art.

CHALLENGE

Plan a day to wear a new fashion look that reflects readiness, focus, and excitement.

ART CHALLENGE #7

SILENT ART

Utilize meditation, mindfulness, and quiet time, etc. to represent the Chosen Life principle through silent art.

CHALLENGE

Visualize yourself at the height of your destiny (i.e. purpose) work. Visualize what it looks-feels-sounds like.

JANUARY 24

CALLED

"The 'layman' need never think of his humbler task as being inferior to that of his minister. Let every man abide in the calling wherein he is called and his work will be as sacred as the work of the ministry. It is not what a man does that determines whether his work is sacred or secular, it is why he does it. The motive is everything. Let a man sanctify the Lord God in his heart and he can thereafter do no common act." — A.W. Tozer

How do you remain humble when people insist on giving you praise, acknowledgement, and encouragement? Who should get full credit for your gifts, talents, and accomplishments? Why?

_____
_____
_____
_____
_____
_____
_____

Ephesians 2:8-9 "For by grace you have been saved through faith. And this is not your own doing; it is the gift of God, not a result of works, so that no one may boast." ESV

JANUARY 25

CALLED

"One good deed is worth more than a thousand brilliant theories. Let us not wait for large opportunities, or for a different kind of work, but do just the things we "find to do" day by day."
— Charles Haddon Spurgeon

How will you remind yourself that your calling brings both preferred and non-preferred tasks? Are these tasks created equal? Are small and large opportunities equally valuable experiences?

_____
_____
_____
_____
_____
_____
_____
_____

2 Timothy 2:20-21 "Now in a great house there are not only vessels of gold and silver but also of wood and clay, some for honorable use, some for dishonorable. Therefore, if anyone cleanses himself from what is dishonorable, he will be a vessel for honorable use, set apart as holy, useful to the master of the house, ready for every good work." ESV

JANUARY 26

CALLED

"It's important to understand that at every point of opposition to who we are or to what God has called us to do, we are presented with the options of either conforming and giving in, or standing our ground and becoming stronger in who God has made us to be" — Gabriel Wilson

How has the calling required you to either conform or give in?
How have you had to stand your ground or become stronger in your identity?

_____
_____
_____
_____
_____
_____
_____
_____
_____

Joshua 1:9 "Have I not commanded you? Be strong and courageous. Do not be frightened, and do not be dismayed, for the Lord your God is with you wherever you go." ESV

CALLED

"We are all priests before God, there is no such distinction as 'secular or sacred.' In fact, the opposite of sacred is not secular; the opposite of sacred is profane. In short, no follower of Christ does secular work. We all have a sacred calling."

— Ravi Zacharias

How is your current work (i.e. career, job, vocation, hobby) sacred or profane (i.e. spiritual or non-spiritual)? Who or what influences the environment? What will you do differently, stop doing, or start doing?

_____
_____
_____
_____
_____
_____
_____
_____

1 Peter 2:5 "You yourselves like living stones are being built up as a spiritual house, to be a holy priesthood, to offer spiritual sacrifices acceptable to God through Jesus Christ." ESV

JANUARY 28

CALLED

"No one was ever called by God to greater suffering than God's only begotten Son." ~R.C. Sproul

How has your calling caused you to suffer and/or experience joy? How does this pain, hurt, or loss compare to the biggest sacrifice ever known?

_____
_____
_____
_____
_____
_____
_____
_____
_____

2 Timothy 2:8-12 "Remember Jesus Christ, risen from the dead, the offspring of David, as preached in my gospel, for which I am suffering, bound with chains as a criminal. But the word of God is not bound! Therefore I endure everything for the sake of the elect, that they also may obtain the salvation that is in Christ Jesus with eternal glory. The saying is trustworthy, for: If we have died with him, we will also live with him; if we endure, we will also reign with him;" ESV

JANUARY 29

CALLED

"Thus, when you wake up in the morning, called by God to be a self again, if you want to know who you are, watch your feet. Because where your feet take you, that is who you are."
~Frederick Buechner

How do your feet represent who you are?
Where are you going and who you are moving towards? Why?
Are you moving away from your power source (i.e. light) as the day develops?

_____
_____
_____
_____
_____
_____
_____
_____
_____
_____

Psalm 119:105 "Your word is a lamp to my feet and a light to my path." ESV

JANUARY 30

CALLED

"I think in my world of religion, you're called to preach or you don't preach. Called by God to preach. I never been ordained by God to preach the gospel. I have a calling, it's called to perform and sing." ~Johnny Cash

How has a legalistic or religious mentality hindered you from understanding your true calling? How has the plan and purpose for your life (i.e. predestination) been impacted by this mentality? How will you move forward?

_____
_____
_____
_____
_____
_____
_____
_____
_____

Ephesians 1:4-6 "In love He predestined us for adoption to Himself as sons through Jesus Christ, according to the purpose of His will, to the praise of His glorious grace, with which He has blessed us in the Beloved." ESV

JANUARY 31

CALLED

"What God is doing today is calling people out of the world for His name. Whether they come from the Muslim world, or the Buddhist world, or the Christian world, or the non-believing world, they are members of the body of Christ because they've been called by God. They may not even know the name of Jesus, but they know in their hearts they need something that they don't have and they turn to the only light they have and I think they're saved and they're going to be with us in heaven." ~Billy Graham

How have you witnessed diverse people from diverse backgrounds being called to serve in unique ways? Who was offended? Why?

_____
_____
_____
_____
_____
_____
_____

Galatians 3:27 "For as many of you as were baptized into Christ have put on Christ. There is neither Jew nor Greek, there is neither slave nor free, there is no male and female, for you are all one in Christ Jesus." ESV

FEBRUARY

Key Principle #2: Challenged

WHY ME? NOW? THIS?

CHALLENGED

Why do problems seem to multiply like stubborn weeds? They sprout up in your personal garden only to 'triple-dog dare' you to remove them at your own risk. So - you brace yourself. You risk defeat and the potential loss of your peace, time or energy. You need to survive, but you don't want the weeds to take over and kill the harvest. You want to remain focused on the positive outcome. So you work harder. You uproot one weed only to provoke three more to grow in its place the next day. Go figure!

Why does conflict catch us by surprise? We may be caught off guard because we really don't like to speak to the harsh reality. Challenges are extremely RUDE!!! They pop-up with no warning or invitation, just like weeds! By the time you realize what's happening, you're in the middle of a storm. A storm that's flooding your garden and quenching the toxic thirst of the weeds. So now what?

Want to grow new skills or be a better leader? Focus on mastering YOU! Challenges are not meant to crush you. They are opportunities for you to assess your present skills and build stamina.

When offense, guilt, shame, grief, death, disappointment, betrayal, addiction, bad news, disease, or a life threatening diagnosis occur, there will be no announcement before the visit. Brace yourself the best way possible. Gleam how you show up. You may not be in control of the circumstance, but you are always in control of your response. Your influence is priceless. Invest!!!

CHALLENGED: AFFIRMATION

ME, MYSELF, & I

I am confident that challenges are opportunities to boomerang my mind, heart, and feet back towards my core values. I understand that I am a unique individual growing and evolving in different ways, speeds and realms. I will stand up, fight every circumstance and address issues by utilizing effective problem-solving strategies and skills.

WE

We agree that challenges are opportunities to redirect our minds, hearts, and feet back towards our core values. We understand that we are two unique individuals growing and evolving in different ways, speeds, and realms. We will stand up, unite, and fight every circumstance and issue by utilizing effective problem-solving strategies and skills.

ART CHALLENGE #1

VISUAL ART

Utilize photography, painting, digital media, sketching, sculpture, collage, crafts, etc. to represent the Chosen Life principle through visual art.

CHALLENGE

Create a vision board or list of 10 images that reflect you as a new and improved person. A person living a purpose-driven life.

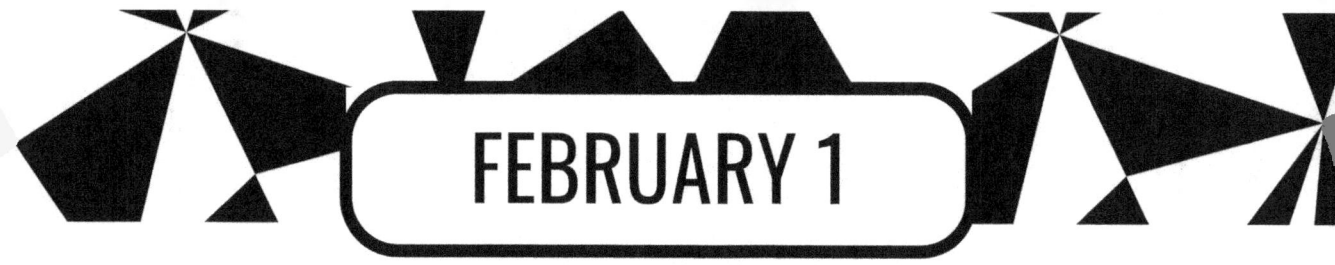

FEBRUARY 1

CHALLENGED

"Obstacles are what you see when you take your eye off your goal." –Anonymous

How will you stay focused when problems compete for your attention?

_____
_____
_____
_____
_____
_____
_____
_____
_____
_____
_____

James 1:2-4 "Count it all joy, my brothers, when you meet trials of various kinds, for you know that the testing of your faith produces steadfastness. And let steadfastness have its full effect, that you may be perfect and complete, lacking in nothing." ESV

FEBRUARY 2

CHALLENGED

"Everything negative-pressure, challenges-is all an opportunity for me to rise." -Kobe Bryant

Will you rise or recede when negativity, pressure, and problems develop? Why? How?

_____
_____
_____
_____
_____
_____
_____
_____
_____
_____
_____
_____
_____
_____

Romans 8:28 "And we know that for those who love God all things work together for good, for those who are called according to His purpose." ESV

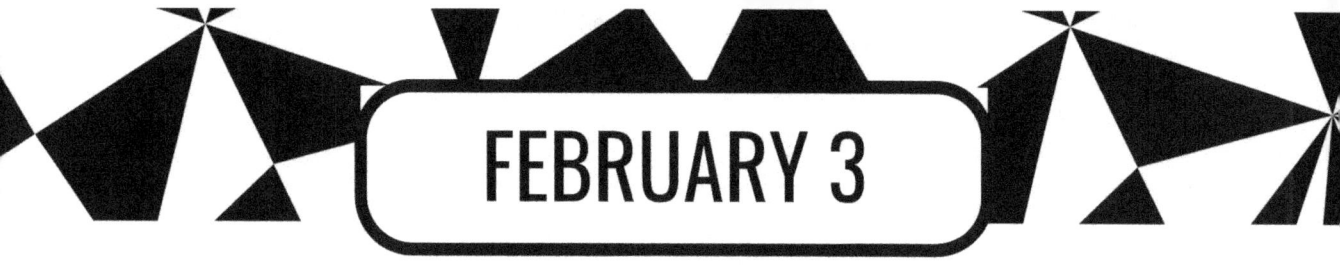

FEBRUARY 3

CHALLENGED

"There will always be obstacles and challenges that stand in your way. Building mental strength will help you develop resilience to those potential hazards so you can continue on your journey to success." ~Amy Morin

Do roadblocks stop you from moving forward, slow you down, or help you to become more creative? Why? How?

_____
_____
_____
_____
_____
_____
_____
_____
_____
_____

Hebrews 10:35 "Therefore do not throw away your confidence, which has a great reward." ESV

FEBRUARY 4

CHALLENGED

"Believe in yourself, take on your challenges, dig deep within yourself to conquer fears. Never let anyone bring you down. You got to keep going." ~Chantal Sutherland

What are the barriers that hold you back, keep you quiet and/or steal your joy? How?

_____
_____
_____
_____
_____
_____
_____
_____
_____
_____
_____

Isaiah 57:14 "And it shall be said, "Build up, build up, prepare the way, remove every obstruction from my people's way." ESV

FEBRUARY 5

CHALLENGED

"Being in control of your life and having realistic expectations about your day-to-day challenges are the keys to stress management, which is perhaps the most important ingredient to living a happy, healthy and rewarding life." ~Marilu Henner

Does bad stress (i.e. distress) or good stress (i.e. eustress) rule your life? Why or why not? What will you do about it?

_____
_____
_____
_____
_____
_____
_____
_____
_____
_____
_____
_____

Philippians 4:13 "I can do all things through Him who strengthens me." ESV

FEBRUARY 6

CHALLENGED

"We rise to challenges, we will meet them, we're well prepared for them, we'll get through them and we'll emerge on the other side stronger." ~Rishi Sunak

What are some past challenges and obstacles you've overcome? What did you learn about yourself? How did you grow?

_____
_____
_____
_____
_____
_____
_____
_____

2 Corinthians 12:8-10 "Three times I pleaded with the Lord about this, that it should leave me. But he said to me, "My grace is sufficient for you, for my power is made perfect in weakness." Therefore I will boast all the more gladly of my weaknesses, so that the power of Christ may rest upon me. For the sake of Christ, then, I am content with weaknesses, insults, hardships, persecutions, and calamities. For when I am weak, then I am strong." ESV

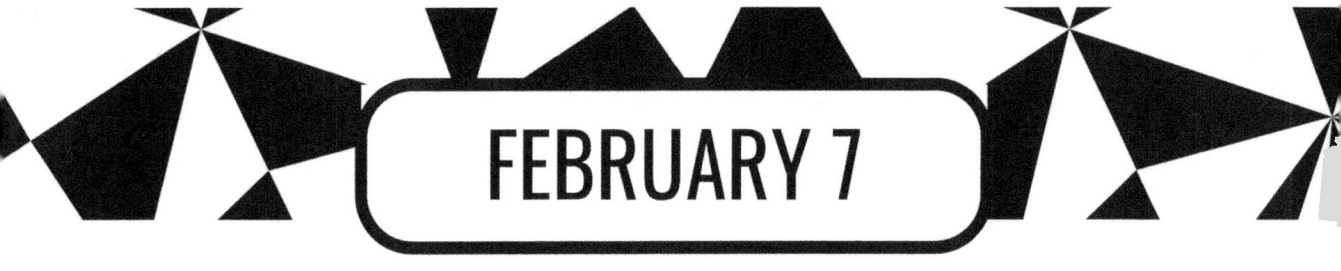

FEBRUARY 7

CHALLENGED

"Together we can face any challenges as deep as the ocean and as high as the sky." ~Sonia Gandhi

Who can you depend on to partner with you during struggles and/or when issues arise? Why? Why is it dangerous to face hardship alone?

___

Romans 14:13 "Therefore let us not pass judgment on one another any longer, but rather decide never to put a stumbling block or hindrance in the way of a brother." ESV

ART CHALLENGE #2

WORD ART

Utilize acrostic poetry, short stories, word cloud, etc. to represent the Chosen Life principle through word art.

CHALLENGE

Design word art that represents conflict that may occur while doing purpose work. Include why the issues will not stop you.

ART CHALLENGE #3

MOVEMENT ART

Utilize dance, human twister poses, acting, etc. to represent the Chosen Life principle through movement art.

CHALLENGE

Create movement art that represents thriving in the midst of a storm.

FEBRUARY 8

CHALLENGED

"Just as we develop our physical muscles through overcoming opposition - such as lifting weights - we develop our character muscles by overcoming challenges and adversity." ~Stephen Covey

What is your physical health regimen? What is your mental health regimen? How does your regimen help you combat your challenges?

_____
_____
_____
_____
_____
_____
_____
_____
_____
_____

I Corinthians 9:27 "But I discipline my body and keep it under control, lest after preaching to others I myself should be disqualified." ESV

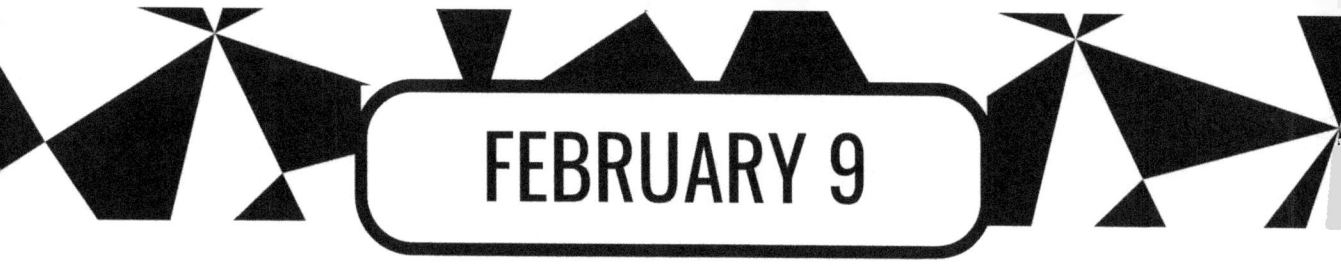

FEBRUARY 9

CHALLENGED

"Common sense would suggest that having ability, like being smart, inspires confidence. It does, but only while the going is easy. The deciding factor in life is how you handle setbacks and challenges. People with a growth mindset welcome setbacks with open arms." ~Travis Bradberry

How do you respond when things don't go according to plan? How flexible are you with your vision and process? How will you improve?

_____
_____
_____
_____
_____
_____
_____
_____
_____

Psalm 37:23-24 "The steps of a man and woman are established by the Lord, when they delight in his way; though they fall, they shall not be cast headlong, for the Lord upholds their hand." ESV

FEBRUARY 10

CHALLENGED

"I believe that every single one of us, celebrity or not, has a responsibility to get involved in trying to make a difference in the world. Our generation faces many challenges, some of which were passed on to us by the past generations, but it's up to us to find solutions today so that we don't keep passing our problems on." ~Shakira

What did you learn from your foundational family about dealing with challenges and difficulties? Do you plan to continue in it or change it? Why or why not?

_____
_____
_____
_____
_____
_____
_____
_____

Matthew 28:18-19 "And Jesus came and said to them, "All authority in heaven and on earth has been given to me. Go therefore and make disciples of all nations, baptizing them in the name of the Father and of the Son and of the Holy Spirit." ESV

FEBRUARY 11

CHALLENGED

"Success is due to our stretching to the challenges of life. Failure comes when we shrink from them." ~John C. Maxwell

What is your definition of success?
How do failure and difficulties factor into it? Do they help or harm?

_____
_____
_____
_____
_____
_____
_____
_____
_____
_____
_____
_____

Proverbs 16:3 "Commit your work to the Lord, and your plans will be established." ESV

FEBRUARY 12

CHALLENGED

"It's lack of faith that makes people afraid of meeting challenges, and I believed in myself." ~Muhammad Ali

Do you need to believe in yourself to accomplish what you want to do? Are you relying on the belief of others to carry your dreams to the finish line?
Why or Why Not?

___
___
___
___
___
___
___
___
___
___

Hebrews 11:6 "And without faith it is impossible to please God, for whoever would draw near to God must believe that He exists and that He rewards those who seek him." ESV

FEBRUARY 13

CHALLENGED

"Sometimes the hurdles aren't really hurdles at all. They're welcome challenges and tests." ~Paul Walker

What are your strengths and talents during conflict?
How were they developed?
How do you use them to help? Is your practice helpful or harmful?

_____
_____
_____
_____
_____
_____
_____
_____
_____
_____

1 Corinthians 10:13 "No temptation has overtaken you that is not common to man. God is faithful, and He will not let you be tempted beyond your ability, but with the temptation He will also provide the way of escape, that you may be able to endure it." ESV

FEBRUARY 14

CHALLENGED

"Life's challenges are not supposed to paralyze you, they're supposed to help you discover who you are."
~Bernice Johnson Reagon

Have you ever felt 'stuck' in life? If so, when did it happen and how did you get out of it? If you currently feel 'stuck', when did it start and how have you tried to get out of it? Make a list of options and ask wise people for ideas.

_____
_____
_____
_____
_____
_____
_____
_____
_____

Proverbs 3:5-6 "Trust in the Lord with all your heart, and do not lean on your own understanding. In all your ways acknowledge Him, and He will make straight your paths." ESV

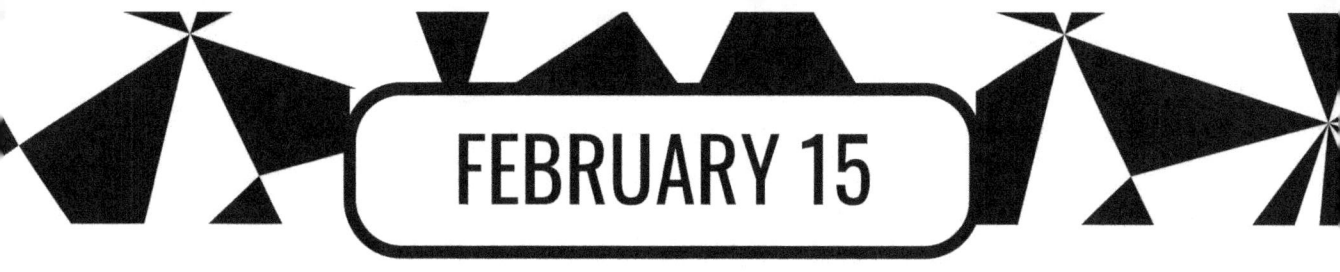

CHALLENGED

"You should never view your challenges as a disadvantage. Instead, it's important for you to understand that your experience facing and overcoming adversity is actually one of your biggest advantages." ~Michelle Obama

What is your perspective on your challenges and difficulties?
Is your perspective helping or harming?
How can you turn adversity into advantage?

_____
_____
_____
_____
_____
_____
_____
_____
_____
_____

Isaiah 41:13 "For I, the Lord your God, hold your right hand; it is I who say to you, "Fear not, I am the one who helps you." ESV

ART CHALLENGE #4

MUSIC ART

Utilize instrumentals, lyrics, or diverse genres to represent the Chosen Life principle through music art.

CHALLENGE

Identify music that represents strength in the middle of a storm. A warrior's chant or victory anthem.

ART CHALLENGE #5

CULINARY ART

Utilize cooking, baking, drink design, and the 5 senses (sight, touch, smell, taste, and hearing) to represent the Chosen Life principle through culinary art.

CHALLENGE

Visit a restaurant that has your ideal warrior's meal on the menu. A meal that empowers and strengthens.

FEBRUARY 16

CHALLENGED

"I think we're going to the moon because it's in the nature of the human being to face challenges. It's by the nature of his deep inner soul... we're required to do these things just as salmon swim upstream." ~Neil Armstrong

What is your 'impossible' dream(s)? Why is it hard? When did you first have it? What makes it largely difficult (i.e. mentality, people, access to resources)?

_____
_____
_____
_____
_____
_____
_____
_____
_____
_____

Matthew 19:26 "But Jesus looked at them and said, "With man this is impossible, but with God all things are possible." ESV

FEBRUARY 17

CHALLENGED

"Every project is an opportunity to learn, to figure out problems and challenges, to invent and reinvent." ~David Rockwell

What is your strategy for solving problems?
How and what can people count on you to do in difficult situations?

_____
_____
_____
_____
_____
_____
_____
_____
_____
_____
_____
_____

Genesis 50:20 "As for you, you meant evil against me, but God meant it for good, to bring it about that many people should be kept alive, as they are today." ESV

FEBRUARY 18

CHALLENGED

"Teachers can change lives with just the right mix of chalk and challenges." ~Joyce Meyer

What teacher(s) had the biggest influence on your life? Why?
How did the chalk and challenges help you?
How do you use those same lessons today?

_____
_____
_____
_____
_____
_____
_____
_____
_____
_____
_____

Habakkuk 2:3 "For still the vision awaits its appointed time; it hastens to the end—it will not lie. If it seems slow, wait for it; it will surely come; it will not delay." ESV

FEBRUARY 19

CHALLENGED

"The key to life is accepting challenges. Once someone stops doing this, he's dead." ~Bette Davis

Have you ever run away from a challenge? When? Why? What was it? What were the missed opportunities? Have you regained the missed lesson(s)?

_____
_____
_____
_____
_____
_____
_____
_____
_____
_____
_____

Romans 5:3-5 "Not only that, but we rejoice in our sufferings, knowing that suffering produces endurance, and endurance produces character, and character produces hope, and hope does not put us to shame, because God's love has been poured into our hearts through the Holy Spirit who has been given to us." ESV

FEBRUARY 20

CHALLENGED

"There is strength in numbers, but organizing those numbers is one of the great challenges." ~John C. Mather

Do you have any mentors or coaches you turn to for guidance and advice? How many do you have? How often do you speak to them? Why or why not? What are their areas of strength?

_____
_____
_____
_____
_____
_____
_____
_____
_____
_____
_____
_____
_____
_____

Proverbs 11:14 "Where there is no guidance, a people fall, but in an abundance of counselors there is safety." ESV

FEBRUARY 21

CHALLENGED

"We all have challenges. We have to face them, embrace them, defy them, and conquer them." ~Victoria Arlen

What is your daily practice for problems and circumstances? Do you face them, embrace them, defy them or conquer them? How?

_____
_____
_____
_____
_____
_____
_____
_____
_____
_____
_____
_____
_____

Psalm 118:13 "I was pushed hard, so that I was falling, but the Lord helped me." ESV

FEBRUARY 22

CHALLENGED

"Our ability to handle life's challenges is a measure of our strength of character." ~Les Brown

Is my character on trial because of how I handle hardship? Should I be defined by my response and/or reaction to pain, hurt and trauma? Why or why not?

_____
_____
_____
_____
_____
_____
_____
_____
_____
_____

James 1:12 "Blessed is the one who remains steadfast under trial, for when they have stood the test they will receive the crown of life, which God has promised to those who love him." ESV

FEBRUARY 23

CHALLENGED

"If I could talk to my younger self, I would just say that the path to great things is filled with a lot of stumbles, suffering, and challenges along the way. But if you have the right attitude and know that hard times will pass – and you get up each time – you will reach your destination." –Jonny Kim

What 3 things would you tell your younger self about dealing with challenges?

_____
_____
_____
_____
_____
_____
_____
_____

Proverbs 1:32-33 "For the simple are killed by their turning away, and the complacency of fools destroys them; but whoever listens to (wisdom) will dwell secure and will be at ease, without dread of disaster." ESV

ART CHALLENGE #6

FASHION ART

Utilize clothing, make-up, or jewelry art, interior design work, etc. to represent the Chosen Life principle through fashion art.

CHALLENGE

Look in your closet and pick out a "warrior's uniform".

ART CHALLENGE #7

SILENT ART

Utilize meditation, mindfulness, and quiet time, etc. to represent the Chosen Life principle through silent art.

CHALLENGE

Visualize 3 of the most important things that matter during troubled times.

FEBRUARY 24

CHALLENGED

"Challenges make you discover things about yourself that you never really knew." ~Cicely Tyson

What things did you learn about yourself the last time you faced challenges and difficulties? Would you place these traits under your areas of strengths or opportunity for growth list?

_____
_____
_____
_____
_____
_____
_____
_____
_____
_____
_____

Deuteronomy 31:6 "Be strong and courageous. Do not fear or be in dread of them, for it is the Lord your God who goes with you. He will not leave you or forsake you." ESV

FEBRUARY 25

CHALLENGED

"Optimistic people play a disproportionate role in shaping our lives. Their decisions make a difference; they are inventors, entrepreneurs, political and military leaders – not average people. They got to where they are by seeking challenges and taking risks." ~Daniel Kahneman

Which characteristics define risk takers?
Do you consider yourself a risk taker? Why or why not?
What are 3 ways you can strengthen this muscle (i.e. skill)?

___

Hebrews 12:1 "Therefore, since we are surrounded by so great a cloud of witnesses, let us also lay aside every weight, and sin which clings so closely, and let us run with endurance the race that is set before us." ESV

FEBRUARY 26

CHALLENGED

"We need diversity of thought in the world to face the new challenges." ~Tim Berners-Lee

Are you a divergent thinker? Why or why not? Do creative thinkers live happier, healthier more hopeful lives? Why or why not?

_____
_____
_____
_____
_____
_____
_____
_____
_____
_____
_____
_____

Colossians 3:2 "Set your minds on things that are above, not on things that are on earth." ESV

CHALLENGED

"Life is a series of punches. It presents a lot of challenges. It presents a lot of hardship, but the people that are able to take those punches and able to move forward are the ones that really do have a lot of success and have a lot of joy in their life and have a lot of stories to tell, too." ~Josh Turner

What is the hardest challenge you have ever faced? When was it? How did you overcome it? What was your fight strategy? Was there any collateral damage?

_____
_____
_____
_____
_____
_____
_____
_____
_____
_____

Romans 3:23 "For all have sinned and fall short of the glory of God." ESV

FEBRUARY 28

CHALLENGED

"The truth is that stress doesn't come from your boss, your kids, your spouse, traffic jams, health challenges, or other circumstances. It comes from your thoughts about these circumstances." ~Andrew J. Bernstein

What are some of the things that the voices in your head tell you when you're facing challenges? Is the voice positive or negative? Is it kind or cruel?

___

___

___

___

___

___

___

___

___

___

Isaiah 26:3 "You keep in perfect peace those whose mind is stayed on you, because they trust in you." ESV

FEBRUARY 29

CHALLENGED

"I wanted to live the life, a different life. I didn't want to go to the same place every day and see the same people and do the same job. I wanted interesting challenges." ~Harrison Ford

Is variety the "spice of life?" How will you explore a diverse palette of flavors? What have you noticed about people who limit their experiences?

___
___
___
___
___
___
___
___
___
___
___
___

Jeremiah 29:11 "For I know the plans I have for you, declares the Lord, plans for welfare and not for evil, to give you a future and a hope." ESV

MARCH

Key Principle #3: Changed

METAMORPHOSIS REVEALED

CHANGED

Change is inevitable. Well, at least that's what they say. However, time has proven this to be an immutable fact: The industrial revolution. The digital age. In-person board meetings. Virtual conferences. Hip-Hop Symphonies. Movies shown out of chronological order. Armed security at churches. Meatless Mondays. Passenger Trains. Driverless vehicles (i.e. DRIVERLESS VEHICLES!)

The reality is that even when we make the choice to stand still, life will not hesitate to move forward with or without our permission. "Who moved my cheese?" meets "Do I have to accept this technical update"? This stark realization can often result in frustration and bitterness if we're not honest with ourselves. Honest about what? The truth that we're actually afraid because we feel like we are not in control of our lives.

Does our ability to determine our circumstances minimize our ability to determine our attitude and behavior? If change is inevitable, what is our role in the process? Believe it or not, you DO have a say - maybe not in what change looks like, but possibly in the ramifications of the outcome.

Spoiler alert: Change is coming. How are you getting ready?

CHANGED: AFFIRMATION

ME, MYSELF, & I

I will be transformed through mental metamorphosis. I am dedicated to showing up stronger, wiser, and better during each personal life cycle and circumstance. I will remain committed to developing resilience strategies, tools, and skills in order to build myself up.

WE

We will be transformed through mental growth. We are dedicated to showing up stronger, wiser, and better during each marital life cycle and circumstance. We will remain committed to developing resilience strategies, tools, and skills in order to build up one another and strengthen our union.

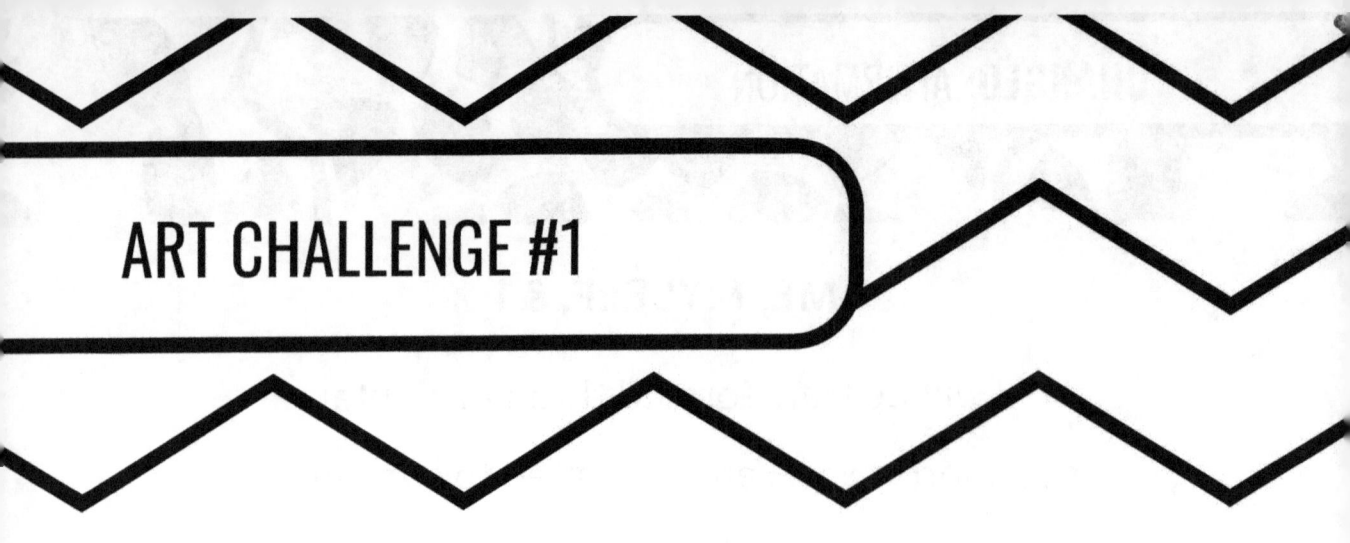

ART CHALLENGE #1

VISUAL ART

Utilize photography, painting, digital media, sketching, sculpture, collage, crafts, etc. to represent the Chosen Life principle through visual art.

CHALLENGE

Create a vision board or list of images that reflect you as a new person.

MARCH 1

CHANGED

"Change will not come if we wait for some other person or some other time. We are the ones we've been waiting for. We are the change that we seek." ~Barack Obama

Do you embrace change? Do you pursue it or does it pursue you? Do you treat change like a friend or a foe? Why? Explain.

_____
_____
_____
_____
_____
_____
_____
_____
_____
_____
_____

Proverbs 3:5-6 "Trust in the Lord with all your heart, and do not lean on your own understanding. In all your ways acknowledge Him, and He will make straight your paths." ESV

MARCH 2

CHANGED

"To improve is to change; to be perfect is to change often."
~Winston Churchill

How do you exercise the muscle of change? Where does change occur most frequently (i.e. head, heart, or hands and feet)? Explain.

_____
_____
_____
_____
_____
_____
_____
_____
_____
_____
_____
_____

Psalm 51:10 "Create in me a clean heart, O God, and renew a right spirit within me." ESV

MARCH 3

CHANGED

"If you change the way you look at things, the things you look at change." ~Wayne Dyer

How do you see the world? Does this perspective help or hurt? Heal or Hinder? Provide hope or horror? Where does this perspective come from and how can you enhance the view?

_____
_____
_____
_____
_____
_____
_____
_____
_____
_____
_____
_____

Daniel 2:20-21 "Blessed be the name of God forever and ever, to whom belong wisdom and might. He changes times and seasons; He removes kings and sets up kings; He gives wisdom to the wise and knowledge to those who have understanding;" ESV

MARCH 4

CHANGED

"If there is no struggle, there is no progress. (i.e. change)
~Frederick Douglass

How can your struggles drive change for you and others? Does difficulty promote innovation and curiosity or vice versa?

_____
_____
_____
_____
_____
_____
_____
_____
_____
_____
_____
_____
_____

Revelation 21:5 "And He who was seated on the throne said, "Behold, I am making all things new." ESV

MARCH 5

CHANGED

"There is nothing permanent except change." ~Heraclitus

Think of 3 people who regularly reject change. What is their level of happiness, productivity, and independence? Is this perspective beneficial or a barrier?

___

Ecclesiastes 3:1 "For everything there is a season, and a time for every matter under heaven." ESV

MARCH 6

CHANGED

"God grant me the serenity to accept the things I cannot change, the courage to change the things I can, and the wisdom to know the difference." ~Reinhold Niebuhr

Are courage and acceptance both skills required to change? Why or why not? What is your secret sauce to change? Explain.

_____
_____
_____
_____
_____
_____
_____
_____
_____
_____

1 John 1:9 "If we confess our sins, He is faithful and just to forgive us our sins and to cleanse us from all unrighteousness." ESV

MARCH 7

CHANGED

"Everyone thinks of changing the world, but no one thinks of changing himself." —Leo Tolstoy

Do you agree or disagree with the idea that you can change the world by changing yourself? Explain.

_____
_____
_____
_____
_____
_____
_____
_____
_____
_____

Titus 3:3-6 "For we ourselves were once foolish, disobedient, led astray, slaves to various passions and pleasures, passing our days in malice and envy, hated by others and hating one another. But when the goodness and loving kindness of God our Savior appeared, He saved us, not because of works done by us in righteousness, but according to His own mercy, by the washing of regeneration and renewal of the Holy Spirit, whom He poured out on us richly through Jesus Christ our Savior." ESV

ART CHALLENGE #2

WORD ART

Utilize acrostic poetry, short stories, word cloud, etc. to represent the Chosen Life principle through word art.

CHALLENGE

Write an acrostic poem using the word "changed."

(i.e. C.H.A.N.G.E.D.)

ART CHALLENGE #3

MOVEMENT ART

Utilize dance, human twister poses, acting, etc. to represent the Chosen Life principle through movement art.

CHALLENGE

Tap 3 different areas of your body that have positively changed as an act of gratitude.

MARCH 8

CHANGED

"The only way to make sense out of change is to plunge into it, move with it and join the dance." ~Alan Watts

Does change require us to be a professional marathon runner or a local neighborhood jogger? Do you prefer to confront and embrace change with speed and urgency or a slow and steady approach? Why?

___

Philippians 3:21 "Who will transform our lowly body to be like His glorious body, by the power that enables Him even to subject all things to Himself." ESV

MARCH 9

CHANGED

"Not everything that is faced can be changed. But nothing can be changed until it is faced." ~James Baldwin

What do you see in your community, home, or on your job that can be changed for the better? Explain how they may be enhanced.

_____
_____
_____
_____
_____
_____
_____
_____
_____
_____
_____

Romans 12:2 "Do not be conformed to this world, but be transformed by the renewal of your mind, that by testing you may discern what is the will of God, what is good and acceptable and perfect." ESV

MARCH 10

CHANGED

"Money and success don't change people; they merely amplify what is already there." ~Will Smith

Does money change people or do people change how they treat you when you get money? Explain.

_____
_____
_____
_____
_____
_____
_____
_____
_____
_____
_____
_____
_____
_____

1 Timothy 6:10 "For the love of money is a root of all kinds of evils. It is through this craving that some have wandered away from the faith and pierced themselves with many pangs." ESV

MARCH 11

CHANGED

"If you want to make enemies, try to change something."
~Woodrow Wilson

Have you or a friend gained enemies by being a change agent? Why?
How did you navigate this unfortunate experience?
Would you do anything differently? Explain.

_____
_____
_____
_____
_____
_____
_____
_____
_____
_____
_____

Exodus 23:22 "But if you carefully obey His voice and do all that I say, then I will be an enemy to your enemies and an adversary to your adversaries." ESV

MARCH 12

CHANGED

"Change is hard because people overestimate the value of what they have and underestimate the value of what they may gain by giving that up." ~James Belasco and Ralph Stayer

How have you recently given to something that did not benefit you? Is it possible to gain more by giving more? If so, how?

_____
_____
_____
_____
_____
_____
_____
_____
_____

Exodus 23:22 "But if you carefully obey His voice and do all that I say, then I will be an enemy to your enemies and an adversary to your adversaries." ESV

MARCH 13

CHANGED

"Just because everything is different doesn't mean anything has changed." ~Irene Peter

Have you ever been surprised that things were uniquely different even though there wasn't evidence of actual change? What elements are actually needed to experience change and transformation?

_____
_____
_____
_____
_____
_____
_____
_____
_____
_____

Jeremiah 2:11 "Has a nation changed its gods, even though they are no gods? But my people have changed their glory for that which does not profit." ESV

MARCH 14

CHANGED

"Change is inevitable. Change is constant." ~Benjamin Disraeli

How have you had to exercise your change muscle the past few weeks? Explain. Has it enhanced or hindered? Has it been hard or seamless? What is your process or coping strategy?

_____
_____
_____
_____
_____
_____
_____
_____
_____
_____
_____
_____

Hebrews 7:12 "For when there is a change in the priesthood, there is necessarily a change in the law as well." ESV

MARCH 15

CHANGED

"Progress is a nice word. But change is its motivator. And change has its enemies." ~Robert Kennedy

How can change be both a motivator and an enemy? Make a list of how change has become an enemy and/or a motivator for you and the people you love?

_____
_____
_____
_____
_____
_____
_____
_____
_____
_____

Micah 7:5-6 "Put no trust in a neighbor; have no confidence in a friend; guard the doors of your mouth from her who lies in your arms; for the son treats the father with contempt, the daughter rises up against her mother, the daughter- in-law against her mother-in-law; a man's enemies are the men of his own house." ESV

ART CHALLENGE #4

MUSIC ART

Utilize instrumentals, lyrics, or diverse genres to represent the Chosen Life principle through music art.

CHALLENGE

Turn on a positive yet random music playlist. Listen for the change and transitions.

ART CHALLENGE #5

CULINARY ART

Utilize cooking, baking, drink design, and the 5 senses (sight, touch, smell, taste, and hearing) to represent the Chosen Life principle through culinary art.

CHALLENGE

Identify a drink that represents "change" and a fresh start.

MARCH 16

CHANGED

"Culture does not change because we desire to change it. Culture changes when the organization is transformed, the culture reflects the realities of people working together every day."
~Frances Hesselbein

What is your reality? Is your environment changing because you are or are you changing because your environment is changing?
Which is the leader of change? Explain.

_____
_____
_____
_____
_____
_____
_____
_____
_____
_____

James 1:22 "But be doers of the word, and not hearers only, deceiving yourselves." ESV

MARCH 17

CHANGED

"The greatest discovery of all time is that a person can change [their] future by merely changing [their] attitude" ~Oprah Winfrey

How has changing your attitude changed your life? Make a list of how this has occurred in your life. How do you desire to change your attitude further?

_____
_____
_____
_____
_____
_____
_____
_____
_____
_____
_____
_____

Ecclesiastes 8:1 "Who is like the wise? And who knows the interpretation of a thing? A man's wisdom makes his face shine, and the hardness of his face is changed." ESV

MARCH 18

CHANGED

"They always say time changes things, but you actually have to change them yourself." ~Andy Warhol

Have you relied on time as a key element for initiating change? How did this belief system disprove or prove to be accurate?

_____
_____
_____
_____
_____
_____
_____
_____
_____
_____
_____

Psalm 90:12 "So teach us to number our days that we may get a heart of wisdom." ESV

MARCH 19

CHANGED

"The world as we have created it is a process of our thinking. It cannot be changed without changing our thinking."
~Albert Einstein

Have your thoughts truly created and attracted the very things you envision? If so, how? How will you use this process to attract positivity and prevent negativity? Explain.

_____
_____
_____
_____
_____
_____
_____
_____
_____
_____
_____

Proverbs 23:7 "For as he thinketh in his heart, so is he."

MARCH 20

CHANGED

"The key to change is to let go of fear." ~Rosanne Cash

How does fear (i.e. false evidence, emotions, and environments appearing real) keep you from accomplishing your life dreams and goals? Does fear need to be conquered before you can truly embrace change?

_____
_____
_____
_____
_____
_____
_____
_____
_____
_____
_____
_____
_____
_____

1 John 4:18 "There is no fear in love, but perfect love casts out fear." ESV

MARCH 21

CHANGED

"Change your opinions, keep to your principles; change your leaves, keep intact your roots." ~Victor Hugo

How do you determine which aspects of your character to change and which to keep? Reflect which things you have changed and how they have benefited you? What are the principles that will remain the same and why?

_____
_____
_____
_____
_____
_____
_____
_____
_____
_____
_____
_____

Philippians 1:6 "And I am sure of this, that He who began a good work in you will bring it to completion at the day of Jesus Christ." ESV

MARCH 22

CHANGED

"Vision without action is merely a dream. Action without vision just passes the time. Vision with action can change the world."
~Joel A. Barker

How have you been placed on earth to make a difference?
What things have you been called to change? Explain.

_____
_____
_____
_____
_____
_____
_____
_____
_____
_____

James 2:26 "For as the body apart from the spirit is dead, so also faith apart from works is dead." ESV

CHANGED

"Change is the law of life and those who look only to the past or present are certain to miss the future." ~John F. Kennedy

What does it mean to be change driven? Does it mean to look to the past, present, or future? How will you utilize all three to help the others flourish?

_____
_____
_____
_____
_____
_____
_____
_____
_____
_____
_____
_____
_____

Proverbs 23:18 "Surely there is a future, and your hope will not be cut off." ESV

ART CHALLENGE #6

FASHION ART

Utilize clothing, make-up, or jewelry art, interior design work, etc. to represent the Chosen Life principle through fashion art.

CHALLENGE

Pick a new palette of makeup or an outfit that represents the new you. Take a selfie.

ART CHALLENGE #7

SILENT ART

Utilize meditation, mindfulness, and quiet time, etc. to represent the Chosen Life principle through silent art.

CHALLENGE

Meditate on the beauty and discomfort that new beginnings bring (e.g. Spring time).

MARCH 24

CHANGED

"The world hates change, yet it is the only thing that has brought progress." –Charles Kettering

Is making progress worth fighting for in order to gain change? How will you encourage yourself and your loved ones to become comfortable being uncomfortable? Explain.

_____
_____
_____
_____
_____
_____
_____
_____
_____
_____

Romans 7:15 "For I do not understand my own actions. For I do not do what I want, but I do the very thing I hate." ESV

MARCH 25

CHANGED

"I cannot say whether things will get better if we change; what I can say is they must change if they are to get better."
~George C. Lichtenberg

What are the possible consequences of not moving forward with necessary changes? What will be gained? What will be lost?

_____
_____
_____
_____
_____
_____
_____
_____
_____
_____

Hebrews 8:6 "But as it is, Christ has obtained a ministry that is as much more excellent than the old as the covenant He mediates is better, since it is enacted on better promises." ESV

MARCH 26

CHANGED

"Every successful organization has to make the transition from a world defined primarily by repetition to one primarily defined by change. This is the biggest transformation in the structure of how humans work together since the Agricultural Revolution." ~Bill Drayton

Who are your potential partners in your quest for change?
What makes them a worthy ally?
How can they hold you accountable for the changes you want to make?

_____
_____
_____
_____
_____
_____
_____
_____
_____

Amos 3:3 "Do two walk together, unless they have agreed to meet?" ESV

MARCH 27

CHANGED

"Change is a normal part of our lives, but it's uncomfortable for the vast majority of people because it makes them feel like they've lost control. Do you remember a time when you felt like things were being done to you that you had no control over? That's how they may feel now. In every way you can, let them know that you can relate to that." –Mary Jo Asmus

What role does control play in change? Do you willingly relinquish it or fight to keep it? What has been your experience in balancing control and change?

_____
_____
_____
_____
_____
_____
_____
_____

Matthew 6:34 "Therefore do not be anxious about tomorrow, for tomorrow will be anxious for itself. Sufficient for the day is its own trouble." ESV

MARCH 28

CHANGED

"Change cannot be put on people. The best way to instill change is to do it with them. Create it with them." ~Lisa Bodell

Is it your responsibility to convince others to change? Why or Why not? If Yes, how do you communicate this to them? If No, what is your response or action?

___
___
___
___
___
___
___
___
___
___
___
___
___

Proverbs 13:20 "Whoever walks with the wise becomes wise, but the companion of fools will suffer harm." ESV

CHANGED

"As dealing with change becomes a regular activity, leading it becomes a skill to hone, an internal capacity to master."
~Arnaud Henneville

What does "adopting a lifestyle of change" look like?
What are the benefits? What are the challenges?

___

Ecclesiastes 9:11 "I saw that under the sun the race is not to the swift, nor the battle to the strong, nor bread to the wise, nor riches to the intelligent, nor favor to those with knowledge, but time and chance happen to them all." ESV

MARCH 30

CHANGED

"Change hurts. It makes people insecure, confused, and angry. People want things to be the same as they've always been because that makes life easier. But, if you're a leader, you can't let your people hang on to the past." ~Richard Marcinko

Does change make stability and consistency unrealistic? Why or why not?

_____
_____
_____
_____
_____
_____
_____
_____
_____
_____
_____

Isaiah 33:6 "And He will be the stability of your times, abundance of salvation, wisdom, and knowledge." ESV

MARCH 31

CHANGED

"The reality is that the only way change comes is when you lead by example." ~Anne Wojcicki

What are some of the obstacles you've overcome during previous changes? What did you learn from them? What did you learn about you?

_____
_____
_____
_____
_____
_____
_____
_____
_____
_____

Romans 5:3-5 "Not only that, but we rejoice in our sufferings, knowing that suffering produces endurance, and endurance produces character, and character produces hope, and hope does not put us to shame, because God's love has been poured into our hearts through the Holy Spirit who has been given to us." ESV

APRIL

Key Principle #4: Heart Healthy

LOVE... FORGIVE... YADA-YADA!!!!

HEART-HEALTHY

At the risk of a heart disease diagnosis, would you work hard to lose weight, change your diet or sign up for a new gym membership? Sensitive to the circumstances, would you start an intense exercise regimen with a personal trainer? Most likely! You might spare no expense and exhaust all options to save your own life. But what if the primary "key" to your heart health was to unlock the vulnerable (i.e. willingness to show weakness) process of forgiveness, love, and respect. Sound absurd? Well... it's not!

Why are we so easy to "ask" for forgiveness yet so slow and reluctant to "grant it" to others?" Ouch!!! Perhaps you are the exception to this common behavior? Maybe you haven't done anything offensive that warrants your request?
Well, you are definitely a rare gem! "What does forgiveness have to do with heart health?" Well... EVERYTHING!!!

A healthy heart is directly linked to forgiveness. Forgiveness is tied to love. Love is connected to respect. It is an act of grace and mercy to the giver and receiver. When done correctly, "forgiveness can reduce the risk of heart attack by improving cholesterol levels, sleep, reducing pain, blood pressure, diabetes, anxiety levels, depression, and stress."

 A healthy heart gives love, grace, mercy, and shows respect with healthy boundaries and expectations for self and others. Health is manifest in the mind, mouth, hands, feet, and body. The heart is the most essential muscle in the body. Why not give it what it needs to function at it's healthiest capacity?

HEART-HEALTHY: AFFIRMATION

ME, MYSELF, & I

I will outline and define love and respect in order to combine and create healthy boundaries and expectations. I will demonstrate knowledge, understanding, love, respect, and forgiveness without limits during each life cycle.

WE

We will outline and define love and respect in order to combine and create healthy boundaries and expectations. We will demonstrate knowledge, understanding, love, respect, and forgiveness without limits during each life cycle.

ART CHALLENGE #1

VISUAL ART

Utilize photography, painting, digital media, sketching, sculpture, collage, crafts, etc. to represent the Chosen Life principle through visual art.

CHALLENGE

Create a drawing or sketch that reflects the value of setting healthy boundaries to protect your heart.

APRIL 1

HEART HEALTHY

"God speaks in the silence of the heart. Listening is the beginning of prayer". ~Mother Teresa

How do you listen to your heart? What do you need to do in order to be silent and concentrate? What would be the benefit and/or benefits?

_____
_____
_____
_____
_____
_____
_____
_____
_____
_____
_____
_____

Psalm 90:12-"So teach us to number our days that we may get a heart of wisdom." ESV

APRIL 2

HEART HEALTHY

"Don't be pushed around by the fears in your mind. Be led by the dreams in your heart." ~Roy T. Bennett

Are you guided by the fear of the mind or the dreams of your heart? Which do you give the most power and why? How has this behavior helped you and/or hurt your personal development?

_____
_____
_____
_____
_____
_____
_____
_____
_____
_____

Matthew 15:18-20 "But what comes out of the mouth proceeds from the heart, and this defiles a person. For out of the heart come evil thoughts, murder, adultery, sexual immorality, theft, false witness, slander. These are what defile a person." ESV

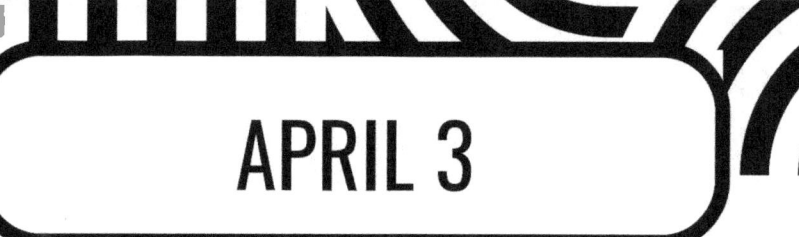

APRIL 3

HEART HEALTHY

"Prayer is not asking. It is a longing of the soul. It is daily admission of one's weakness. It is better in prayer to have a heart without words than words without a heart."
— *Mahatma Gandhi*

Do you have a heart without words or words without a heart? What are 2-3 messages that have been resonating with you recently and why? What does it mean and how will you utilize the internal message?

_____
_____
_____
_____
_____
_____
_____
_____

Psalm 19:14 "Let the words of my mouth and the meditation of my heart be acceptable in your sight, O Lord, my rock and my redeemer." ESV

APRIL 4

HEART HEALTHY

"Pursue what catches your heart, not what catches your eyes."
— *Roy T. Bennet*

Are you guided most by your eyes or your heart? Why or why not? What is the benefit or consequence or your choices? Would you follow the same path if given a second chance?

_____
_____
_____
_____
_____
_____
_____
_____
_____
_____

1 Samuel 16:7-"But the Lord said to Samuel, "Do not look on his appearance or on the height of his stature, because I have rejected him. For the Lord sees not as man sees: man looks on the outward appearance, but the Lord looks on the heart." ESV

APRIL 5

HEART HEALTHY

"Start each day with a positive thought and a grateful heart."
— Roy T. Bennet

How do you begin your day? What are 2-3 things that you do to demonstrate being grateful? What are the benefits or barriers?

_____
_____
_____
_____
_____
_____
_____
_____
_____
_____
_____
_____
_____

Matthew 5:8-"Blessed are the pure in heart, for they shall see God." ESV

APRIL 6

HEART HEALTHY

"Believe in your heart that you're meant to live a life full of passion, purpose, magic, and miracles." — Roy T. Bennett

What do you believe that you were meant to do, where were you meant to go, and who were you meant to impact? Have you experienced the fulfillment of your passion and purpose? Have you experienced magic and miracles?

_____
_____
_____
_____
_____
_____
_____
_____
_____
_____
_____

Proverbs 3:5-6 "Trust in the Lord with all your heart, and do not lean on your own understanding. In all your ways acknowledge Him, and He will make straight your paths" ESV

APRIL 7

HEART HEALTHY

"To give my heart means...the risk is high and jackpot isn't guaranteed. Access is a privilege that awakens the 5 senses, kills the ego, and puts evil behavior on trial. To win, is to define dignity, respect, care, and consideration granularly and to forgive blindly."
—Charmaine Jennings, Ed.S.

"If you gave someone your heart and they died, did they take it with them? Did you spend the rest of forever with a hole inside you that couldn't be filled?" — Jodi Picoult

_____
_____
_____
_____
_____
_____
_____
_____

Proverbs 4:23-"Keep your heart with all vigilance, for from it flow the springs of life." ESV

ART CHALLENGE #2

WORD ART

Utilize acrostic poetry, short stories, word cloud, etc. to represent the Chosen Life principle through word art.

CHALLENGE

Write a forgiveness letter that will help your heart self-heal.

ART CHALLENGE #3

MOVEMENT ART

Utilize dance, human twister poses, acting, etc. to represent the Chosen Life principle through movement art.

CHALLENGE

Take a nature walk. Observe and document the relaxed and peaceful vibes all around.

APRIL 8

HEART HEALTHY

"The heart is an arrow. It demands aim to land true."
— Leigh Bardugo

How much effort have you invested to heal your heart? To gain the desires of your heart? To give the matters of your heart a voice? What was the outcome and would you do it again? Are you open to explore the health of your heart in the following way deeper and with intention?

_____
_____
_____
_____
_____
_____
_____
_____
_____
_____

Jeremiah 17:9-10 "The heart is deceitful above all things, and desperately sick; who can understand it? "I the Lord search the heart and test the mind, to give every man according to his ways, according to the fruit of his deeds." ESV

APRIL 9

HEART HEALTHY

"One love, one heart, one destiny." — Robert Marley

Can you have one love, one heart, and one destiny? Why or why not? How can having multiple loves, hearts, and destinies bound or benefit? Explain.

_____
_____
_____
_____
_____
_____
_____
_____
_____
_____
_____
_____
_____

Psalm 86:11 "Teach me your way, O Lord, that I may walk in your truth; unite my heart to fear your name." ESV

APRIL 10

HEART HEALTHY

"Suffering has been stronger than all other teaching, and has taught me to understand what your heart used to be. I have been bent and broken, but – I hope – into a better shape." — Charles Dickens

How can suffering help you to understand at deeper levels? How does a broken heart build resilience, self-reflection and sharpen a thirst for personal growth and development? Explain.

_____
_____
_____
_____
_____
_____
_____
_____
_____
_____
_____
_____

Psalm 51:17 "The sacrifices of God are a broken spirit; a broken and contrite heart, O God, you will not despise." ESV

APRIL 11

HEART HEALTHY

"When the heart speaks, the mind finds it indecent to object."
— *Milan Kundera*

What does it mean to speak from the heart? When was the last time you heard a speaker convey a message from the heart? What characteristics stood out about the speaker(s)? Why was it compelling? Explain.

_____
_____
_____
_____
_____
_____
_____
_____
_____
_____
_____

Proverbs 12:25 "Anxiety in a man's heart weighs him down, but a good word makes him glad." ESV

APRIL 12

HEART HEALTHY

"I know I am but summer to your heart, and not the full four seasons of the year." — Edna St. Vincent Millay

Does a healthy heart expect loved ones to give them 365 days a year of their time and attention? Must love consume, possess, or demand all of your time and attention? Are boundaries the key to a healthy heart or the barrier that withholds trust and transparency?

_____
_____
_____
_____
_____
_____
_____
_____
_____
_____
_____
_____

Psalm 51:10 "Create in me a clean heart, O God, and renew a right spirit within me." ESV

APRIL 13

HEART HEALTHY

"The heart has its reasons which reason knows not." — Blaise Pascal

Can you make both an emotional heart decision and a rational mind decision at the same time? Think of a time when you or a friend had this dilemma. How did they make the decision? Which area gave more or sacrificed more? Explain.

_____
_____
_____
_____
_____
_____
_____
_____
_____
_____
_____
_____
_____

Philippians 4:7 "And the peace of God, which surpasses all understanding, will guard your hearts and your minds in Christ Jesus." ESV

APRIL 14

HEART HEALTHY

"You are not rich until you have a rich heart." — Roy T. Bennett

What does it mean to have a rich heart? How would life be more valuable with this condition? What are the benefits or barriers? Explain.

_____
_____
_____
_____
_____
_____
_____
_____
_____
_____
_____

Hebrews 10:22 "Let us draw near with a true heart in full assurance of faith, with our hearts sprinkled clean from an evil conscience and our bodies washed with pure water." ESV

APRIL 15

HEART HEALTHY

"Do you think, because I am poor, obscure, plain and little, I am soulless and heartless? You think wrong! – I have as much soul as you, – and full as much heart! And if God had gifted me with some beauty and much wealth, I should have made it as hard for you to leave me, as it is now for me to leave you!"

— *Charlotte Brontë*

Does your socioeconomic status determine your heart's capacity to love, empathize, or think beyond your own basic needs and desires? Does wealth, beauty, fame, and allure cause you to tolerate maltreatment, bad behavior, and people who lack integrity? Why or why not? Explain.

_____
_____
_____
_____
_____
_____
_____
_____

Proverbs 21:2-"Every way of a man is right in his own eyes, but the Lord weighs the heart." ESV

ART CHALLENGE #4

MUSIC ART

Utilize instrumentals, lyrics, or diverse genres to represent the Chosen Life principle through music art.

CHALLENGE

Create a 5-8 song playlist to establish a morning routine that energizes.

ART CHALLENGE #5

CULINARY ART

Utilize cooking, baking, drink design, and the 5 senses (sight, touch, smell, taste, and hearing) to represent the Chosen Life principle through culinary art.

CHALLENGE

Find a new recipe and cook a healthy meal or explore a healthy restaurant and treat yourself.

APRIL 16

HEART HEALTHY

"When you are sorrowful look again in your heart, and you shall see that in truth you are weeping for that which has been your delight." — Kahlil Gibran

How can having a healthy heart help you see delight where others see sorrow, or purpose where others see pain? Do you or someone you know experience this level of heart health? Explain the benefits and/or barriers.

_____
_____
_____
_____
_____
_____
_____
_____
_____
_____

Proverbs 21:2 "Every way of a man is right in his own eyes, but the Lord weighs the heart." ESV

APRIL 17

HEART HEALTHY

"The only calibration that counts is how much heart people invest, how much they ignore their fears of being hurt or caught out or humiliated. And the only thing people regret is that they didn't live boldly enough, that they didn't invest enough heart, didn't love enough. Nothing else really counts at all." — Ted Hughes

A healthy heart is a "bold" heart. Think about a time when you or someone was bold and demonstrated. What was the cost of their investment? What did you/they lose or gain in the process? Make a list and audit the high price of becoming heart healthy. Can you ever gain without losing or lose without gaining something? Why or why not?

_____
_____
_____
_____
_____
_____
_____
_____

Psalm 37:4 "Delight yourself in the Lord, and He will give you the desires of your heart." ESV

APRIL 18

HEART HEALTHY

"I have not broken your heart – you have broken it; and in breaking it, you have broken mine." — Emily Brontë

Who do you hold responsible for your broken heart? Who holds ownership? Is it ever okay to blame the condition of our heart on others? How does this choice benefit or hinder personal growth and development?

_____
_____
_____
_____
_____
_____
_____
_____
_____
_____

Psalm 73:26 "My flesh and my heart may fail, but God is the strength of my heart and my portion forever." ESV

APRIL 19

HEART HEALTHY

"Thou hast made us for thyself, O Lord, and our heart is restless until it finds its rest in thee." — Augustine of Hippo

A healthy heart has peace. How do you gain, maintain, and cultivate peace in your heart? Who is involved in this process? How consistent, reliable, and strategic is this person? Explain.

___

John 14:27 "Peace I leave with you; my peace I give to you. Not as the world gives do I give to you. Let not your hearts be troubled, neither let them be afraid." ESV

APRIL 20

HEART HEALTHY

"Goodbyes are only for those who love with their eyes. Because for those who love with heart and soul there is no such thing as separation." — Rumi

How can you build relationships that last forever? How can a person love with their heart and soul but without their eyes? Which is better and/or more sustaining? Explain.

_____
_____
_____
_____
_____
_____
_____
_____
_____

John 15:12-13 "This is my commandment, that you love one another as I have loved you. Greater love has no one than this, that someone lay down his life for his friends." ESV

APRIL 21

HEART HEALTHY

"Do what you love, love what you do, and with all your heart give yourself to it." — Roy T. Bennett

A healthy heart is balanced. How can you work hard, play hard, and live a life of abundance simultaneously?
Are you willing the set a goal to enhance this area of your life?
Why or why not? What would this plan-of-action look-feel-sound like?

_____
_____
_____
_____
_____
_____
_____
_____
_____
_____
_____

Matthew 6:21-"For where your treasure is, there your heart will be also." ESV

APRIL 22

HEART HEALTHY

"Somewhere, far down, there was an itch in his heart, but he made it a point not to scratch it. He was afraid of what might come leaking out." — *Markus Zusak*

A healthy heart embraces truth even if it causes pain. How do you respond to your intuition telling you that something is good, bad, right, or wrong? Do you embrace the good and ignore the bad? Has this helped or hurt you and will you continue this practice? Why or why not?

_____
_____
_____
_____
_____
_____
_____
_____

Hebrews 4:12 "For the word of God is living and active, sharper than any two-edged sword, piercing to the division of soul and of spirit, of joints and of marrow, and discerning the thoughts and intentions of the heart." ESV

APRIL 23

HEART HEALTHY

"Do not let arrogance go to your head and despair to your heart; do not let compliments go to your head and criticisms to your heart; do not let success go to your head and failure to your heart." — Roy T. Bennett

How do you determine whether to distribute positive and negative input between the head and the heart (e.g. arrogance, despair, compliments, criticisms, success, and failure)? Are you satisfied with your process? How could it be improved, refined, or revamped? Explain.

_____
_____
_____
_____
_____
_____
_____
_____

Joel 2:13-"And rend your hearts and not your garments." Return to the Lord your God, for He is gracious and merciful, slow to anger, and abounding in steadfast love; and He relents over disaster." ESV

ART CHALLENGE #6

FASHION ART

Utilize clothing, make-up, or jewelry art, interior design work, etc. to represent the Chosen Life principle through fashion art.

CHALLENGE

Wear a pair of shoes that symbolize and represent your efforts to be heart healthy.

ART CHALLENGE #7

SILENT ART

Utilize meditation, mindfulness and quiet time, etc. to represent the Chosen Life principle through silent art.

CHALLENGE

Take a power nap or a restoration break.

APRIL 24

HEART HEALTHY

"Sometimes all a person wants is an empathetic ear; all he or she needs is to talk it out. Just offering a listening ear and an understanding heart for his or her suffering can be a big comfort." — Roy T. Bennett

How does the power of being listened to with an empathetic ear and being understood provide comfort? When was the last time you truly felt heard? What made it so special? Explain.

_____
_____
_____
_____
_____
_____
_____
_____

1 Corinthians 13:4-7 "Love is patient and kind; love does not envy or boast; it is not arrogant or rude. It does not insist on its own way; it is not irritable or resentful; it does not rejoice at wrongdoing, but rejoices with the truth. Love bears all things, believes all things, hopes all things, endures all things." ESV

APRIL 25

HEART HEALTHY

"I could hear my heart beating. I could hear everyone's heart. I could hear the human noise we sat there making, not one of us moving, not even when the room went dark." — Raymond Carver

How do you respond when you are afraid? In a dark setting and unable to see? Held against your will? Unfortunately, millions of people throughout history have been captured and enslaved. Would you choose the consequence of flat-lining in the pursuit of freedom or choose a heartbeat and life with oppression? Why or why not?

_____
_____
_____
_____
_____
_____
_____
_____
_____
_____

Psalm 34:18 "The Lord is near to the brokenhearted and saves the crushed in spirit." ESV

APRIL 26

HEART HEALTHY

"You have a good heart. Sometimes that's enough to see you safe wherever you go. But mostly, it's not." — Neil Gaiman

What does it mean to have a good heart? Is a good heart all you need to be safe in this world? Why or why not?

___

Proverbs 3:1-2 "My child, do not forget my teaching, but let your heart keep my commandments, for length of days and years of life and peace they will add to you." ESV

APRIL 27

HEART HEALTHY

"One ought to hold on to one's heart; for if one lets it go, one soon loses control of the head too." — Friedrich Nietzsche

What would your life look-feel-sound-be like if you lost your heart (i.e. emotions) and/or head (i.e. mind)? Does the head and the heart work as a team? If you lose one do you automatically lose the other? Why or why not?

_____
_____
_____
_____
_____
_____
_____
_____
_____
_____
_____
_____

Matthew 22:37 "You shall love the Lord your God with all your heart and with all your soul and with all your mind." ESV

APRIL 28

HEART HEALTHY

"Anger, resentment, and jealousy doesn't change the heart of others— it only changes yours." — Shannon Alder

Describe the last time that you were angry, resentful, or jealous. How did it impact your life and the people you care about? How do/did they experience you in these moments? Did it negatively impact the person who offended you or did it negatively impact the experiences that your loved ones had with you?

_____
_____
_____
_____
_____
_____
_____
_____
_____
_____

Ezekiel 36:26 "And I will give you a new heart, and a new spirit I will put within you. And I will remove the heart of stone from your flesh and give you a heart of flesh." ESV

APRIL 29

HEART HEALTHY

"Listen to God with a broken heart. He is not only the doctor who mends it, but also the father who wipes away the tears."
— Criss Jami

Who do you rely on to heal your broken heart? Who can you call on to wipe away your tears? Is crying and/or grieving an important part of having a healthy heart, why or why not?

_____
_____
_____
_____
_____
_____
_____
_____
_____
_____
_____

Psalm 147:3 "He heals the brokenhearted and binds up their wounds." ESV

APRIL 30

HEART HEALTHY

"Her heart was a secret garden and the walls were very high."
— *William Goldman*

How can you protect your heart without building walls so high that no one can enter or exit, see inside, or provide opportunities for you to look out? What is the consequence of this type of heightened protection? Explain. Does this practice help to cultivate a healthy heart?

_____
_____
_____
_____
_____
_____
_____
_____
_____

Song of Solomon 8:6 "Set me as a seal upon your heart, as a seal upon your arm, for love is strong as death, jealousy is fierce as the grave. Its flashes are flashes of fire, the very flame of the Lord." ESV

MAY

Key Principle #5: Open-Minded

LOOKS BAD, BUT TASTES GOOD!

OPEN-MINDED

Beets. Brussels Sprouts. Rutabaga. Okra. Cauliflower. Broccoli. Squash. The mere mentioning of these foods can mentally transport us back to a formative time in our life, those impressionable years where we begin to learn the difference between likes and dislikes.

The scene - A person we loved and/or trusted sits one of the aforementioned items in front of us for the first time. It was colorful and new, but while our inquisitiveness was alerted, our 'skepticism alarm' was also tripped. We were curious. We were cautious. We were commanded to eat. It didn't take long before the verdict was rendered: We were betrayed. The bitterness of the encounter still reverberates in our taste buds today if we see the culprit's name in a menu.

Do your beliefs and experiences impede more than they inform? Has the risk-taking, adventurous explorer inside of you been relegated to paths with familiar footprints? Yes, you may be safe, but are you satisfied? The nagging feeling of "more" you're sensing is your comfort's inability to silence the voice of your ambition.

If being open-minded had a motto, it would be "consider the possibilities!" What if the Brussels Sprouts were baked with brown sugar instead of boiled? What if the squash was baptized as a casserole? What if the problem wasn't the product, but the process?

LOOKS BAD, BUT TASTES GOOD!

OPEN-MINDED

It's a new day! The sun is coming up. The dew is slowly evaporating. The time has come for you to flip the sign on your mind from 'closed' to 'open'.

OPEN-MINDED: AFFIRMATION

ME, MYSELF, & I

I will seek first to understand and then to be understood. Communication is effective, open, unbiased, objective, and full of innovative ideas and opinions. My thoughts, empathetic ears, and heart work together to learn and encourage. I invite questions that expand my knowledge base and that cultivates patience.

WE

We will seek first to understand and then to be understood. Communication is effective, open, unbiased, objective, and full of innovative ideas and opinions. Our thoughts, empathetic ears, and hearts work together to learn and encourage. We invite questions, which expand our knowledge base and cultivate patience.

ART CHALLENGE #1

VISUAL ART

Utilize photography, painting, digital media, sketching, sculpture, collage, crafts, etc. to represent the Chosen Life principle through visual art.

CHALLENGE

Watch a movie that inspires you.

MAY 1

OPEN-MINDED

"A mind is like a parachute. It doesn't work if it is not open."
— *Frank Zappa*

What types of things spark your curiosity? When are you most open-minded or closed-minded? Why or why not? How does this impact your life?

_____
_____
_____
_____
_____
_____
_____
_____
_____
_____

Romans 8:5-6 "For those who live according to the flesh set their minds on the things of the flesh, but those who live according to the Spirit set their minds on the things of the Spirit. For to set the mind on the flesh is death, but to set the mind on the Spirit is life and peace." ESV

MAY 2

OPEN-MINDED

"Your assumptions are your windows on the world. Scrub them off every once in a while, or the light won't come in."
— Alan Alda

What assumptions do you have about race/ethnicity, religion, socioeconomic status, sex/gender, culture, disability, sexual orientation, and age? How has this mindset helped or hurt? Misguided or Manifest? Minimized or Multiplied? Explain.

_____
_____
_____
_____
_____
_____
_____
_____
_____
_____

Colossians 3:2 "Set your minds on things that are above, not on things that are on earth." ESV

MAY 3

OPEN-MINDED

"Ignorance more frequently begets confidence than does knowledge: it is those who know little, not those who know much, who so positively assert that this or that problem will never be solved by science." — Charles Darwin

Does having an open mind lead you towards humility or confidence? Control or Spontaneity? Peace or Persistence? Explain.

_____
_____
_____
_____
_____
_____
_____
_____
_____
_____

Isaiah 26:3 "You keep him in perfect peace whose mind is stayed on you, because he trusts in you." ESV

MAY 4

OPEN-MINDED

"If someone is able to show me that what I think or do is not right, I will happily change, for I seek the truth, by which no one was ever truly harmed. It is the person who continues in his self-deception and ignorance who is harmed."

— Marcus Aurelius

What is the process that leads you towards open-mindedness? Seek and Find? Trust but Verify? Wait and See or Investigate and Inquire? Explain.

_____
_____
_____
_____
_____
_____
_____
_____
_____

2 Timothy 1:7 "For God gave us a spirit not of fear but of power, love, and sound mind." ESV

MAY 5

OPEN-MINDED

"Those who cannot change their minds cannot change anything."
— *George Bernard Shaw*

When was a time when you had a fixed mind? Why and How did you navigate the circumstances? Who or what was impacted?

_____
_____
_____
_____
_____
_____
_____
_____
_____
_____
_____
_____
_____

2 Corinthians 10:5 "We destroy arguments and every lofty opinion raised against the knowledge of God, and take every thought captive to obey Christ." ESV

MAY 6

OPEN-MINDED

"It is a narrow mind which cannot look at a subject from various points of view." — George Eliot

What have you learned about the power of a narrow mind? What if you were tasked to open and or change someone's mind, how would you begin the process? Explain.

_____
_____
_____
_____
_____
_____
_____
_____
_____
_____

Philippians 2:4-5 "Let each of you look not only to his own interests, but also to the interests of others. Have this mind among yourselves, which is yours in Christ Jesus." ESV

MAY 7

OPEN-MINDED

"It is never too late to give up your prejudices"
— Henry David Thoreau

Do you have any prejudices? What would you do to free your mind from these ideas? How would you replace those ideas with positive accurate ones?

_____
_____
_____
_____
_____
_____
_____
_____
_____
_____
_____

1 Peter 5:8 "Be sober-minded; be watchful. Your adversary the devil prowls around like a roaring lion, seeking someone to devour." ESV

ART CHALLENGE #2

WORD ART

Utilize acrostic poetry, short stories, word cloud, etc. to represent the Chosen Life principle through word art.

CHALLENGE

Write 1-2 positive affirmations and repeat it throughout the day.

ART CHALLENGE #3

MOVEMENT ART

Utilize dance, human twister poses, acting, etc. to represent the Chosen Life principle through movement art.

CHALLENGE

Play a 5 minute workout video or movie clip of your favorite character and mirror their actions and reactions.

MAY 8

OPEN-MINDED

"If you reject the food, ignore the customs, fear the religion, and avoid the people, you might better stay home."
— James A. Michener

Avoiding everything you disagree with is a recipe for being alone, agree or disagree? Does living an abundant life require open-mindedness? Explain.

_____
_____
_____
_____
_____
_____
_____
_____
_____
_____
_____
_____
_____
_____

2 Corinthians 5:17 "Therefore, if anyone is in Christ, he is a new creation. The old has passed away; behold, the new has come." ESV

MAY 9

OPEN-MINDED

"Every now and then a man's mind is stretched by a new idea or sensation, and never shrinks back to its former dimensions."
— Oliver Wendell Holmes Sr.

Once you know better, will you truly do better? Once you truly possess knowledge can you go back to being clueless? Why or why not?

_____
_____
_____
_____
_____
_____
_____
_____
_____
_____
_____
_____

Psalm 119:15 "I will meditate on your precepts and fix my eyes on your ways." ESV

MAY 10

OPEN-MINDED

"Vulnerability is the only authentic state. Being vulnerable means being open, for wounding, but also for pleasure. Being open to the wounds of life means also being open to the bounty and beauty. Don't mask or deny your vulnerability: it is your greatest asset. Be vulnerable: quake and shake in your boots with it. The new goodness that is coming to you, in the form of people, situations, and things can only come to you when you are vulnerable, i.e., open." — Stephen Russell

Is it possible to build a wall, stand behind it, and be seen? How can vulnerability be experienced unless the recipient be willing? Is vulnerability experienced by choice or force? Explain.

_____

_____

_____

_____

_____

_____

Romans 12:2 "Do not be conformed to this world, but be transformed by the renewal of your mind, that by testing you may discern what is the will of God, what is good and acceptable and perfect." ESV

MAY 11

OPEN-MINDED

"When my information changes, I alter my conclusions. What do you do, sir?" — John Maynard Keynes

How well do your conclusions align with facts and information?

_____
_____
_____
_____
_____
_____
_____
_____
_____
_____
_____
_____

1 Peter 1:13 "Therefore, preparing your minds for action, and being sober-minded, set your hope fully on the grace that will be brought to you at the revelation of Jesus Christ." ESV

MAY 12

OPEN-MINDED

"To be even minded is the greatest virtue. Wisdom is to speak the truth and act in keeping with its nature." — Heraclitus

What things help keep your mind steady and grounded?

_____

_____

_____

_____

_____

_____

_____

_____

_____

_____

_____

_____

Philippians 4:8 "Finally, brothers, whatever is true, whatever is honorable, whatever is just, whatever is pure, whatever is lovely, whatever is commendable, if there is any excellence, if there is anything worthy of praise, think about these things." ESV

MAY 13

OPEN-MINDED

"It does take great maturity to understand that the opinion we are arguing for is merely the hypothesis we favor, necessarily imperfect, probably transitory, which only very limited minds can declare to be a certainty or a truth." — Milan Kundera

What experiences have helped to mature your thought process? What are some changes you have seen in your decision making?

_____
_____
_____
_____
_____
_____
_____
_____
_____
_____

Ephesians 4:23-24 "Be renewed in the spirit of your minds and put on the new self." ESV

MAY 14

OPEN-MINDED

"Begin challenging your own assumptions. Your assumptions are your windows on the world. Scrub them off every once in a while or the light won't come in." — Alan Alda

What are some foundational beliefs that you are now questioning? Why?

_____
_____
_____
_____
_____
_____
_____
_____
_____
_____
_____

Proverbs 3:13 "Blessed is the one who finds wisdom, and the one who gets understanding." ESV

MAY 15

OPEN-MINDED

"Despite my firm convictions, I have been always a man who tries to face facts, and to accept the reality of life as new experience and new knowledge unfolds it. I have always kept an open mind, which is necessary to the flexibility that must go hand in hand with every form of intelligent search for truth."
— Malcolm X

What new ideas or concepts have intrigued your mind? How do they compliment or clash with your beliefs?

_____
_____
_____
_____
_____
_____
_____
_____

Psalm 94:11 "The Lord—knows the thoughts of man, that they are but a breath." ESV

ART CHALLENGE #4

MUSIC ART

Utilize instrumentals, lyrics, or diverse genres to represent the Chosen Life principle through music art.

CHALLENGE

Listen to 2-3 songs from a genre of music that is opposite of your normal music regimen.

ART CHALLENGE #5

CULINARY ART

Utilize cooking, baking, drink design, and the 5 senses (sight, touch, smell, taste, and hearing) to represent the Chosen Life principle through culinary art.

CHALLENGE

Explore a diverse cuisine from a different culture, heritage, or background.

MAY 16

OPEN-MINDED

"By all means let's be open-minded, but not so open-minded that our brains drop out." — Richard Dawkins

What are your non-negotiable principles and core values? When did you adopt them? How effective have they been in helping to direct your life?

_____
_____
_____
_____
_____
_____
_____
_____
_____
_____
_____
_____
_____
_____
_____

James 1:8 "A double-minded man is unstable in all his ways." ESV

MAY 17

OPEN-MINDED

"Few people ask from books what books can give us. Most commonly we come to books with blurred and divided minds, asking of fiction that it shall be true, of poetry that it shall be false, of biography that it shall be flattering, of history that it shall enforce our own prejudices. If we could banish all such preconceptions when we read, that would be an admirable beginning." — Virginia Woolf

How often do you read?
What notable books or writings have influenced your value system?

_____
_____
_____
_____
_____
_____
_____
_____

John 20:31 "But these are written so that you may believe that Jesus is the Christ, the Son of God, and that by believing you may have life in His name." ESV

MAY 18

OPEN-MINDED

"Renewal requires opening yourself up to new ways of thinking and feeling" — Deborah Day

When was the last time you opened your mind to a new way of thinking and feeling? What prompted this experience? What was the outcome?

_____
_____
_____
_____
_____
_____
_____
_____
_____
_____
_____
_____

Revelation 21:5 "And He who was seated on the throne said, "Behold, I am making all things new." ESV

MAY 19

OPEN-MINDED

"Always hear others out and remain open-minded; the day you think you know everything is the day you have the most yet to learn." — A.J. Darkholme

What do you think about a person who behaves as a know-it-all? What do you think they set out to gain and why? How do you engage with such individuals? Are there areas where you fit this characteristic as a know-it-all? How do you stay grounded?

_____
_____
_____
_____
_____
_____
_____
_____
_____
_____

Isaiah 1:18 "Come now, let us reason together", says the Lord." ESV

MAY 20

OPEN-MINDED

"The thing is, it's very dangerous to have a fixed idea. A person with a fixed idea will always find some way of convincing himself in the end that he is right." — Atle Selberg

How does a fixed idea minimize the chance for discussion, critical thinking, and collaborative thinking?

_____
_____
_____
_____
_____
_____
_____
_____
_____
_____
_____

Proverbs 1:22 "How long, O simple ones, will you love being simple? How long will scoffers delight in their scoffing and fools hate knowledge?" ESV

MAY 21

OPEN-MINDED

"Beware: open-mindedness will often say, 'Everything is permissible except a sharp opinion." — Criss Jami

Are you open-minded all of the time?
How would you go about entertaining a different perspective?

_____
_____
_____
_____
_____
_____
_____
_____
_____
_____
_____
_____

1 Corinthians 6:12 "All things are permissible, but not all things are helpful." ESV

MAY 22

OPEN-MINDED

"Flexibility requires an open mind and a welcoming of new alternatives." — Deborah Day

How flexible are you in accepting and/or expanding new ideas? What does this look-feel-sound like?

_____
_____
_____
_____
_____
_____
_____
_____
_____
_____
_____
_____

John 14:26 "But the Helper, the Holy Spirit, whom the Father will send in my name, He will teach you all things and bring to your remembrance all that I have said to you." ESV

MAY 23

OPEN-MINDED

"I believe one of the most sacrificial acts of love adoptive parents can do is to give up their preconceptions and agendas about what their child's views "should" be and be open to hear the conflicting emotions and thoughts their child often experiences."
— Sherrie Eldridge

How do you envision supporting your child's critical thinking skills? Do you believe you should motivate or mold how your child thinks? What is your strategy?

_____
_____
_____
_____
_____
_____
_____
_____

I Corinthians 13:11 "When I was a child, I spoke like a child, I thought like a child, I reasoned like a child. When I grew, I gave up childish ways." ESV

ART CHALLENGE #6

FASHION ART

Utilize clothing, make-up, or jewelry art, interior design work, etc. to represent the Chosen Life principle through fashion art.

CHALLENGE

Change a room arrangement (i.e. furniture, resources, etc.,) in order to provide a fresh perspective and to enhance the living experience.

ART CHALLENGE #7

SILENT ART

Utilize meditation, mindfulness and quiet time, etc. to represent the Chosen Life principle through silent art.

CHALLENGE

Review your progress or personal growth and celebrate your achievements internally.

MAY 24

OPEN-MINDED

"Sit down before facts with an open mind. Be prepared to give up every preconceived notion. Follow humbly wherever and to whatever abyss Nature leads or you learn nothing. Don't push out figures when facts are going in the opposite direction."
— *Hyman G. Rickover*

How do you reconcile your opinions with facts? Are you adopting opinions as fact? What are the benefits or barriers of this behavior?

_____
_____
_____
_____
_____
_____
_____
_____

2 Timothy 2:15 "Study to present yourself to God as one approved, a worker who has no need to be ashamed, rightly handling the word of truth." ESV

MAY 25

OPEN-MINDED

"Don't limit yourself, discover new areas of expertise."
— *Sunday Adelaja*

How do you introduce yourself to new ideas, with fear or fearlessness? Do you see new ideas as threats or opportunities?

_____
_____
_____
_____
_____
_____
_____
_____
_____
_____

Ephesians 4:18 "They are darkened in their understanding, alienated from the life of God because of the ignorance that is in them, due to their hardness of heart." ESV

MAY 26

OPEN-MINDED

"I can't afford to say yes to all my staff's desires, but one thing is certain – I can't afford the outrageous cost of not listening to their requests." — John Yokoyama

Who do you listen to and why?
Who does not have access to your ears and why?

_____
_____
_____
_____
_____
_____
_____
_____
_____
_____

Proverbs 2:2 "Making your ear attentive to wisdom and inclining your heart to understanding." ESV

MAY 27

OPEN-MINDED

"If you ever don't see irony, it's because you're not seeing everything." — Eric Hirzel

Are your listening skills global or local? Why or why not? How does global thinking support you in your local relationships?

_____
_____
_____
_____
_____
_____
_____
_____
_____
_____
_____
_____

2 Corinthians 9:8 "And God is able to make all grace abound to you, so that having all sufficiency in all things at all times, you may abound in every good work." ESV

MAY 28

OPEN-MINDED

"A bloated ego at any age is the biggest hurdle for active learning. Excessive self-pride murders open-mind."
— *Krishna Sagar Rao*

Describe a time when your inability to remain open-minded did not serve you well. Why or why not? Explain how.

_____
_____
_____
_____
_____
_____
_____
_____
_____
_____
_____

Proverbs 16:18 "Pride goes before destruction and a haughty spirit before a fall." ESV

MAY 29

OPEN-MINDED

"We see their lack of education as an advantage. It means no one taught them what to think—or how." — Vincent H. O'Neil

Can a formal education be a hindrance to self-development and open-mindedness? How has your education contributed to your mindset?

_____
_____
_____
_____
_____
_____
_____
_____
_____
_____
_____

Isaiah 55:8 "For my thoughts are not your thoughts, neither are your ways my ways, declares the Lord." ESV

MAY 30

OPEN-MINDED

"I believe your tragedies, losses, sorrows, and hurt happen for you not to you. And I bless the thing that broke you down and cracked you open because the world needed you open."
— Rebecca Campbell

How have your hardships impacted your thinking? Were they a benefit or barrier? Have they added or subtracted value? How?

_____
_____
_____
_____
_____
_____
_____
_____
_____
_____

Romans 8:28 "And we know that for those who love God all things work together for good, for those who are called according to his purpose." ESV

MAY 31

OPEN-MINDED

"Technology can stunt the imagination. And human imagination is a resource with limitless potential." — Vincent H. O'Neil

What is your relationship with technology?
How do you maintain a healthy imagination? Can the two co-exist?

_____
_____
_____
_____
_____
_____
_____
_____
_____
_____
_____

Colossians 2:8 "See to it that no one takes you captive by philosophy and empty deceit, according to human tradition, according to the elemental spirits of the world, and not according to Christ." ESV

JUNE

Key Principle #6: Sacrifice & Surrender

REALLY?!... YOU WANT EVEN MORE?

SACRIFICE & SURRENDER

Do any of the following messages sound familiar?

- *"Mom and Dad I need money!"*
- *"Wait. I thought we were friends?"*
- *"I can't explain it right now, but just trust me."*
- *"I know we are short staffed, but hang in there for the team."*
- *"The GPS is telling us to turn left, but I think we should probably turn right."*
- *"Can I move in with you... it will only be for about 2-3 months?"*
- *"It would make me really-really happy if you would do this for me"*

Okay, you can close your mouth now!!! We have so many campaigns competing for our attention, talent, treasure, and time. How do we make better decisions if and/or when to sacrifice and surrender? Besides, so many requests and recommendations come daily. It can be a lot to process and hard to know when to say "yes, no, or not now," especially when our personalities, culture, or life experiences and history can positively or negatively interrupt our reasoning.

To sacrifice means to suffer loss and to surrender means to relinquish control or transfer authority. We are often called to sacrifice or surrender in order to support the personal growth and development of others and ourself. It can be difficult to determine what to do, when, and why?

> **REALLY?!... YOU WANT EVEN MORE?**

SACRIFICE & SURRENDER

SLOW DOWN!!! This is the key to avoiding emotional decision-making. Wait time is highly valuable. It provides decision-making time away from the presence of the person making the request. Fight the need to please. Resist being the hero. This results in victimhood and martyrdom.

Instead - reflect, journal, and ask deeper questions:

- Our *child needs money, but do we need to be the source or just a resource? Advisor? Should the money be given or earned? Will our response actually help or harm?*
- *Is the person who wants me to trust them, capable and responsible enough to handle the weight of the request? What is their personal investment or risk?*
- *Will the support help or provide a false reality or identity? Will I become a deity in their eyes?*
- *Will I prevent them from maturing (i.e. personal growth and development)?*
- *Am I addicted to the rescue mission?*
- *Am I addicted to the coronation ceremony (i.e. the moment when I am crowned, "the savior of the day")?*

Stop and go....check the mirror!!! We mean well when it comes to others and our individual personal growth. But we should face the truth. Are we called to save or to empower? Were we chosen to be the ONLY light in the room or to help awaken the light in others? Let's surrender the need to be the ultimate 'source' and become a 'resource' or vessel of 'support' during the growth process of our loved ones.

SACRIFICE & SURRENDER: AFFIRMATION

ME, MYSELF, & I

I will offer the highest form of love and charity to my community. I will embrace unconditional love, which goes above and beyond. I will keep a pure heart, good conscience, and a strong work ethic regardless of the circumstances. I will be guided by my core values and goals. I will be selfless in order to serve, honor, and protect. I will surrender my need to be right and recognize my fragility and possibility.

WE

We will offer the highest form of love and charity in marriage and within our community. We will embrace unconditional love, which goes above and beyond. We will keep a pure heart, good conscience, strong work ethic, and will to grow regardless of the circumstances. We will be guided by and honor our vows, core values and relationship goals. May we become selfless with a desire to serve, honor, and protect. May we yield our hearts to one another recognizing the fragility and possibilities.

ART CHALLENGE #1

VISUAL ART

Utilize photography, painting, digital media, sketching, sculpture, collage, crafts, etc. to represent the Chosen Life principle through visual art.

CHALLENGE

Create a sketch or digital collage of 2-3 things that you want to surrender to experience joy and happiness.

JUNE 1

SACRIFICE & SURRENDER

"Love is not a feeling of happiness. Love is a willingness to sacrifice." –Michael Novak

How does your expression of love manifest? Is your love expressed as a feeling or willingness to sacrifice? How has this been a benefit or barrier?

_____
_____
_____
_____
_____
_____
_____
_____
_____
_____

Ephesians 5:2 "And walk in love, as Christ loved us and gave Himself up for us, a fragrant offering and sacrifice to God." ESV

JUNE 2

SACRIFICE & SURRENDER

"True love is selfless. It is prepared to sacrifice." ~Sadhu Vaswani

What does it mean to be selfless? How have you been making sacrifices since the start of the year? Can sacrifice effectively be offered in a selfish capacity? If so explain how/why or why not.

_____
_____
_____
_____
_____
_____
_____
_____
_____
_____
_____
_____
_____

John 3:16 "For God so loved the world, that He gave His only Son, that whoever believes in Him should not perish but have eternal life." ESV

JUNE 3

SACRIFICE & SURRENDER

"You can't achieve anything in life without a small amount of sacrifice." ~Shakira

Make a list of 10 sacrifices that you have made that resulted in a huge reward. Would you make the same sacrifices again?

_____
_____
_____
_____
_____
_____
_____
_____
_____
_____
_____
_____

Romans 12:1 "I appeal to you therefore, by the mercies of God, to present your bodies as a living sacrifice, holy and acceptable to God, which is your spiritual worship." ESV

JUNE 4

SACRIFICE & SURRENDER

"A man who was completely innocent, offered himself as a sacrifice for the good of others, including his enemies, and became the ransom of the world. It was a perfect act."
~Mahatma Gandhi

Is there someone whose sacrifices you find admirable? Who are they? What did they do? How do their actions inspire and motivate you?

_____
_____
_____
_____
_____
_____
_____
_____
_____
_____

Romans 5:8 "But God shows His love for us in that while we were still sinners, Christ died for us." ESV

JUNE 5

SACRIFICE & SURRENDER

"I am a member of a team, and I rely on the team, I defer to it and sacrifice for it, because the team, not the individual, is the ultimate champion." ~Mia Hamm

What is the greatest sacrifice someone has ever made for you?
What is the greatest sacrifice you have made for someone else?

_____
_____
_____
_____
_____
_____
_____
_____
_____
_____

John 15:13 "Greater love has no one than this, that someone lay down his life for his friends." ESV

JUNE 6

SACRIFICE & SURRENDER

"One life is all we have and we live it as we believe in living it. But to sacrifice what you are and to live without belief, that is a fate more terrible than dying." ~Joan of Arc

How do your values and principles factor into your support of others? What do you do when an opportunity to sacrifice for someone conflicts with your belief system?

_____
_____
_____
_____
_____
_____
_____
_____
_____
_____

Psalm 51:17 "The sacrifices of God are a broken spirit; a broken and contrite heart, O God, you will not despise." ESV

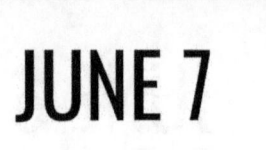

JUNE 7

SACRIFICE & SURRENDER

"When bad men combine, the good must associate; else they will fall one by one, an unpitied sacrifice in a contemptible struggle."
~Edmund Burke

Who are your confidants and allies in your quest to serve others? What qualifies them, from your perspective? How have they encouraged you?

_____
_____
_____
_____
_____
_____
_____
_____
_____
_____
_____

Philippians 2:4 "Let each of you look not only to his own interests, but also to the interests of others." ESV

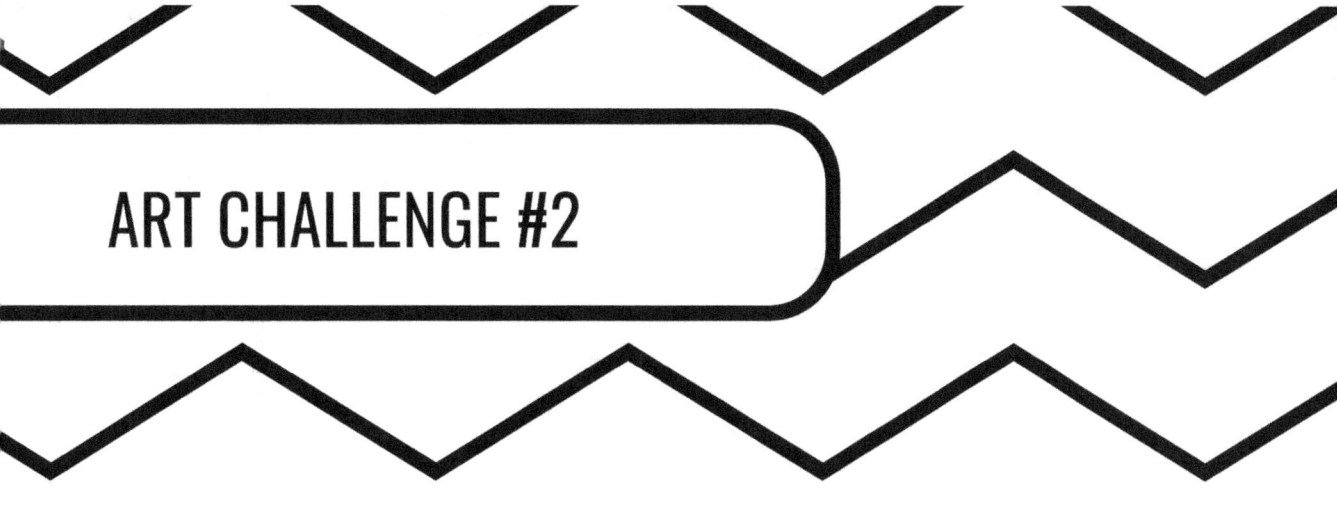

ART CHALLENGE #2

WORD ART

Utilize acrostic poetry, short stories, word cloud, etc. to represent the Chosen Life principle through word art.

CHALLENGE

Give your loved ones 10 minutes of your precious time by sending a few encouraging text messages.

ART CHALLENGE #3

MOVEMENT ART

Utilize dance, human twister poses, acting, etc. to represent the Chosen Life principle through movement art.

CHALLENGE

Make a list of 3 people who you are grateful for because of their sacrifice and/or ability to surrender.

JUNE 8

SACRIFICE & SURRENDER

"Love is not a feeling of happiness. Love is a willingness to sacrifice." ~Michael Novak

What is the relationship between love and sacrifice?
Are they mutually exclusive or two parts of the same whole?

_____
_____
_____
_____
_____
_____
_____
_____
_____
_____
_____
_____

1 John 3:16 "By this we know love, that He laid down His life for us, and we ought to lay down our lives for (others)." ESV

JUNE 9

SACRIFICE & SURRENDER

"People sacrifice the present for the future. But life is available only in the present. That is why we should walk in such a way that every step can bring us to the here and the now."
~Thich Nhat Hanh

How do you balance living for today with preparing for tomorrow? Can both be done simultaneously? What sacrifices are necessary?

_____
_____
_____
_____
_____
_____
_____
_____
_____
_____

2 Corinthians 4:17 "For this light momentary affliction is preparing for us an eternal weight of glory beyond all comparison." ESV

JUNE 10

SACRIFICE & SURRENDER

"Power means happiness; power means hard work and sacrifice."
~Beyonce Knowles

What motivation, energy, or beliefs fuel your sacrifice?
What is your hope or desired outcome?

_____
_____
_____
_____
_____
_____
_____
_____
_____
_____
_____
_____
_____

Luke 9:24 "For whoever would save his life will lose it, but whoever loses his life for my sake will save it." ESV

JUNE 11

SACRIFICE & SURRENDER

"Without the rebellious heart, without people who understand that there's no sacrifice we can make that is too great to retrieve that which we've lost, we will forever be distracted with possessions and trinkets and title." ~Harry Belafonte

What distractions or concerns have challenged you from being selfless? How do you combat them? What have these difficulties taught you about yourself?

_____
_____
_____
_____
_____
_____
_____
_____

Matthew 6:25 "Therefore I tell you, do not be anxious about your life, what you will eat or what you will drink, nor about your body, what you will put on. Is not life more than food, and the body more than clothing?" ESV

JUNE 12

SACRIFICE & SURRENDER

"As long as God gives me strength to work and try to make things real for my children, I'm going to work for it – even if it means making the ultimate sacrifice." –Medgar Evers

When you think of children, what message(s) do you hope they will take from your sacrifices? What are some ways you would like to grow in order to provide an effective example for them?

_____
_____
_____
_____
_____
_____
_____
_____
_____
_____
_____

Matthew 7:11 "If you then, who are evil, know how to give good gifts to your children, how much more will your Father who is in heaven give good things to those who ask Him!" ESV

JUNE 13

SACRIFICE & SURRENDER

"It is my deepest belief that only by giving our lives do we find life. I am convinced that the truest act of courage, the strongest act of manliness is to sacrifice ourselves for others in a totally non-violent struggle for justice." ~Cesar Chavez

In what ways has sacrifice helped you to find and define your life's purpose? What difference has it made?

_____
_____
_____
_____
_____
_____
_____
_____
_____
_____

Galatians 2:20 "I have been crucified with Christ. It is no longer I who live, but Christ who lives in me. And the life I now live in the flesh I live by faith in the Son of God, who loved me and gave Himself for me." ESV

JUNE 14

SACRIFICE & SURRENDER

"I think that the good and the great are only separated by the willingness to sacrifice." ~Kareem Abdul-Jabbar

What old habits or mentalities do you need to confront before moving to the next level? When did you adopt them?
How have they served you? How have you served them?

_____
_____
_____
_____
_____
_____
_____
_____
_____
_____
_____
_____

1 Corinthians 5:7 "Cleanse out the old leaven that you may be a new lump, as you really are unleavened. For Christ, our Passover Lamb, has been sacrificed." ESV

JUNE 15

SACRIFICE & SURRENDER

"How happy had it been for me had I been slain in the battle. It had been far more noble to have died the victim of the enemy than fall a sacrifice to the rage of my friends."
–Alexander the Great

What or who are you willing to die for? Why?

_____
_____
_____
_____
_____
_____
_____
_____
_____
_____

Proverbs 15:3 "The eyes of the Lord are in every place, keeping watch on the evil and the good." ESV

ART CHALLENGE #4

MUSIC ART

Utilize instrumentals, lyrics, or diverse genres to represent the Chosen Life principle through music art.

CHALLENGE

Send an encouraging song to a co-worker, family, or community member who is going through something difficult.

ART CHALLENGE #5

CULINARY ART

Utilize cooking, baking, drink design, and the 5 senses (sight, touch, smell, taste, and hearing) to represent the Chosen Life principle through culinary art.

CHALLENGE

Buy, cook, or share a meal with a person in need.

JUNE 16

SACRIFICE & SURRENDER

"Great leaders are willing to sacrifice the numbers to save the people. Poor leaders sacrifice the people to save the numbers."
~Simon Sinek

Would you categorize yourself as more 'people focused' or 'mission focused'? What contributes to your priority?

_____
_____
_____
_____
_____
_____
_____
_____
_____

Philippians 2:5-8 "Have this mind among yourselves, which is yours in Christ Jesus, who, though He was in the form of God, did not count equality with God a thing to be grasped, but emptied Himself, by taking the form of a servant, being born in the likeness of men. And being found in human form, He humbled Himself by becoming obedient to the point of death, even death on a cross." ESV

JUNE 17

SACRIFICE & SURRENDER

"Freedom does not come without a price. We may sometimes take for granted the many liberties we enjoy in America, but they have all been earned through the ultimate sacrifice paid by so many of the members of our armed forces." –Charlie Dent

What sacrifices have afforded you the life you have now? Who made them? Do you feel a sense of debt to them? If so, what do you owe?

_____
_____
_____
_____
_____
_____
_____
_____
_____

Joel 3:9-10 "Proclaim this among the nations: Consecrate for war; stir up the mighty. Let them draw near; let them come up. Beat your plowshares into swords, and your pruning hooks into spears; let the weak say, "I am a warrior." ESV

JUNE 18

SACRIFICE & SURRENDER

"The reason why many are still troubled, still seeking, still making little forward progress is because they haven't yet come to the end of themselves. We're still trying to give orders, and interfering with God's work within us." — A. W. Tozer

Do you subscribe to the notion of destiny or fate? Why? What is your role and responsibility in your belief?

_____
_____
_____
_____
_____
_____
_____
_____
_____
_____

Luke 9:23 And He said to all, "If anyone would come after me, let him deny himself and take up his cross daily and follow me." ESV

JUNE 19

SACRIFICE & SURRENDER

"Be lost. Give up. Give In. In the end, it would be better to surrender before you begin. Be lost. Be lost and then you will not care if you are ever found." — Victoria Schwab, Vicious

Is there a path or task "calling you" that you've been fighting against? What is it? What is holding you back from yielding to "the call"?

_____
_____
_____
_____
_____
_____
_____
_____
_____
_____

1 Peter 5:6 "Humble yourselves, therefore, under the mighty hand of God so that at the proper time He may exalt you." ESV

JUNE 20

SACRIFICE & SURRENDER

"Reason lost the battle, and all I could do was surrender and accept I was in love." — Paulo Coelho

Describe the relationship between your mind and heart. Which one do you find yourself listening to most? Why?

_____
_____
_____
_____
_____
_____
_____
_____
_____
_____
_____
_____
_____

Proverbs 23:26 "My son, give me your heart, and let your eyes observe my ways." ESV

JUNE 21

SACRIFICE & SURRENDER

"Something amazing happens when we surrender and just love. We melt into another world, a realm of power already within us. The world changes when we change. The world softens when we soften. The world loves us when we choose to love the world."
— Marianne Williamson

Do you believe that how we love ourselves influences how the world loves us? Why or why not?

_____
_____
_____
_____
_____
_____
_____
_____
_____

I John 4:18 "There is no fear in love, but perfect love casts out fear." ESV

JUNE 22

SACRIFICE & SURRENDER

"You cannot fulfill God's purposes for your life while focusing on your own plans." — *Rick Warren*

Who or what have you surrendered to? What led to your decision? How has it impacted your life?

_____
_____
_____
_____
_____
_____
_____
_____
_____
_____
_____
_____
_____

Jeremiah 10:23 "I know, O Lord, that the way of man is not in Himself, that it is not in man who walks to direct His steps." ESV

JUNE 23

SACRIFICE & SURRENDER

"Don't look for peace. Don't look for any other state than the one you are in now; otherwise, you will set up inner conflict and unconscious resistance. Forgive yourself for not being at peace. The moment you completely accept your non-peace, your non-peace becomes transmuted into peace. Anything you accept fully will get you there, will take you into peace. This is the miracle of surrender." — Eckhart Tolle

Do you consider "peace" a place or a state of mind? If a place, what does it look, feel, and sound like? If a state of mind, what are its characteristics?

___

2 Corinthians 12:9 "But He said to me, "My grace is sufficient for you, for my power is made perfect in weakness." Therefore I will boast all the more gladly of my weaknesses, so that the power of Christ may rest upon me." ESV

ART CHALLENGE #6

FASHION ART

Utilize clothing, make-up, or jewelry art, interior design work, etc. to represent the Chosen Life principle through fashion art.

CHALLENGE

Donate articles of clothing (i.e. ties or jackets), books that highlight diversity or other items to a local school in a low-income area.

ART CHALLENGE #7

SILENT ART

Utilize meditation, mindfulness, and quiet time, etc. to represent the Chosen Life principle through silent art.

CHALLENGE

Practice deep breathing and meditation and focus on the sound of your breathing.

JUNE 24

SACRIFICE & SURRENDER

"Now we cannot...discover our failure to keep God's law except by trying our very hardest (and then failing). Unless we really try, whatever we say there will always be at the back of our minds the idea that if we try harder next time we shall succeed in being completely good. Thus, in one sense, the road back to God is a road of moral effort, of trying harder and harder. But in another sense it is not trying that is ever going to bring us home. All this trying leads up to the vital moment at which you turn to God and say, "You must do this. I can't." — C.S. Lewis

In your own words, what does it mean to surrender?
Where did your definition come from? What has been your experience with it?

_____
_____
_____
_____
_____
_____

Luke 18:26-27 "Those who heard it (the conversation w/the Rich Ruler) said, "Then who can be saved?" But he said, "What is impossible with man is possible with God." ESV

JUNE 25

SACRIFICE & SURRENDER

"We are at our most powerful the moment we no longer need to be powerful." — Eric Micha'el Leventhal

Describe 2-3 situations where you truly felt powerful.
Do they all have anything in common?
What do you find interesting about those moments?

_____
_____
_____
_____
_____
_____
_____
_____
_____
_____
_____
_____
_____
_____

I Peter 5:7 "Cast all your cares upon the Lord, because He cares for you." ESV

JUNE 26

SACRIFICE & SURRENDER

"No man is great enough or wise enough for any of us to surrender our destiny to. The only way in which anyone can lead us is to restore to us the belief in our own guidance."
— Henry Miller

Who are some of the people that have helped you to believe in yourself? Who are some of the people that have caused you to doubt yourself? What have you learned about them and yourself?

___

___

___

___

___

___

___

___

Psalm 37:7 "Be still before the Lord and wait patiently for Him; fret not yourself over the one who prospers in his way, over the man who carries out evil devices!" ESV

JUNE 27

SACRIFICE & SURRENDER

"At fifteen, life had taught me undeniably that surrender, in its place, was as honorable as resistance, especially if one had no choice." — Maya Angelou

Is there a relationship between resistance and surrender? How do the two compare and contrast? What has been your experience with each of them?

_____
_____
_____
_____
_____
_____
_____
_____
_____
_____
_____

James 4:8 "Draw near to God, and He will draw near to you. Cleanse your hands, you sinners, and purify your hearts, you double-minded." ESV

JUNE 28

SACRIFICE & SURRENDER

"The greatness of the man's power is the measure of his surrender." — William Booth

What things do you need to relinquish but are struggling to let go? What is the truth about your challenge with these things?

_____
_____
_____
_____
_____
_____
_____
_____
_____
_____
_____
_____
_____

John 15:5 "I am the vine; you are the branches. Whoever abides in me and I in them, they will bear much fruit, for apart from me you can do nothing." ESV

JUNE 29

SACRIFICE & SURRENDER

"Don't despair: despair suggests you are in total control and know what is coming. You don't – surrender to events with hope."
— Alain de Botton

What things are in your circle of control? What things are in your circle of influence? What things are in your circle of concern?
How do you conduct yourself in each circle?

_____
_____
_____
_____
_____
_____
_____
_____
_____
_____

Psalm 9:10 "And those who know your name put their trust in you, for you, O Lord, have not forsaken those who seek you." ESV

JUNE 30

SACRIFICE & SURRENDER

"The more you go with the flow of life and surrender the outcome to God, and the less you seek constant clarity, the more you will find that fabulous things start to show up in your life."

— *Mandy Hale*

What unexpected outcomes have resulted from your willingness to let things go? How has this encouraged or discouraged you in your life path?

_____
_____
_____
_____
_____
_____
_____
_____
_____
_____

Proverbs 3:5-6 "Trust in the Lord with all your heart, and do not lean on your own understanding. In all your ways acknowledge Him, and He will make straight your paths." ESV

JULY

Key Principle #7: Everywhere Matters

Grocery Stores, Coffee Shops, & Bus Stops

EVERYWHERE MATTERS

One of the most popular episodes of the hit show, "Seinfeld" was "The Marine Biologist". In the segment, George Costanza (portrayed by Jason Alexander) pretends to be a marine biologist in order to impress a former crush. The fabrication unravels when the couple encounters a beached whale while on a date. The pantomiming antics of George desperately attempting to embody such a specialist were hilarious and futile. They also succeed in communicating 2 important morals: 1.) Never pretend to be something or someone you're not (see 'Inside Out Before Outside In') and 2.) always be prepared to act in your authenticity.

The weekend may provide us a reprieve from our jobs, but it does not guarantee that we will avoid our "work". Unfortunately, there is no 'break' from you being you. It is possible that life will summon you into action during the most inconvenient times and/or in the most obscure places. Are you willing to lend your skills and expertise outside of your normal business hours? Can you operate in unfamiliar territory or unfriendly confines?

However, bear in mind that this isn't limited to just being a Good Samaritan. In a world that has become increasing anti-social yet social media driven, the willingness to engage in a conversation with a stranger is a radical act. Just imagine the things we can learn from one another when we allow ourselves to be fully present...in the moment. Who knows? What you know and have to say...may actually save my life.

EVERYWHERE MATTERS: AFFIRMATION

Me, Myself, & I

Everywhere I go is an opportunity to directly or indirectly witness to others in and outside of my community. I am an ambassador of my core values and principles. I will utilize my personal life story and marital experiences to enlighten and empower.

WE

Everywhere we go is an opportunity to directly or indirectly witness to others in and outside of our family. We are ambassadors of our core values and principles. We will utilize our personal life story and marital experiences to enlighten and empower.

ART CHALLENGE #1

VISUAL ART

Utilize photography, painting, digital media, sketching, sculpture, collage, crafts, etc. to represent the Chosen Life principle through visual art.

CHALLENGE

Identify 3-5 images that represent the places that mean the most to your growth and development.

JULY 1

EVERYWHERE MATTERS

"When everything hurries everywhere, nothing goes anywhere."
— *Dejan Stojanovic*

What are you in a rush to accomplish?
How much progress have you made? Why or why not?

_____
_____
_____
_____
_____
_____
_____
_____
_____
_____
_____
_____

Philippians 4:6-8 "Do not be anxious about anything, but in everything by prayer and supplication with thanksgiving let your requests be made known to God." ESV

JULY 2

EVERYWHERE MATTERS

"Like a spider in its web, a vibration anywhere is felt everywhere." — *Lois Farfel Stark*

What are some of the things that make you proud? What are your proudest accomplishments? Explain.

_____
_____
_____
_____
_____
_____
_____
_____
_____
_____
_____

Proverbs 19:21 "Many are the plans in the mind of a person, but it is the purpose of the Lord that will stand." ESV

JULY 3

EVERYWHERE MATTERS

"You can see God from anywhere if your mind is set to love and obey Him." — A.W. Tozer

Are you able to love and obey during the most difficult times? Explain why or why not.

_____
_____
_____
_____
_____
_____
_____
_____
_____
_____
_____
_____

1 John 5:3 "For this is the love of God, that we keep His commandments. And His commandments are not burdensome." ESV

JULY 4

EVERYWHERE MATTERS

"Everywhere's a here, isn't it?" — Ali Smith

If you could be anywhere other than where you are, where would you be and why?

_____
_____
_____
_____
_____
_____
_____
_____
_____
_____
_____

Joshua 1:9 "Have I not commanded you? Be strong and courageous. Do not be frightened, and do not be dismayed, for the Lord your God is with you wherever you go." ESV

JULY 5

EVERYWHERE MATTERS

"If you truly love beauty, you will find beauty everywhere."
— Khalid Masood

Can you recall beautiful moments from ugly situations? Explain.

___

Ecclesiastes 3:11 "He (God)h as made everything beautiful in its time." ESV

JULY 6

EVERYWHERE MATTERS

"You are everywhere and yet I am far away from you."
— Nitya Prakash

Who seems to always be a physical presence yet there is a huge distance between you both? Why or why not?

_____
_____
_____
_____
_____
_____
_____
_____
_____
_____
_____
_____

Isaiah 29:13 "And the Lord said: "These people draw near with their mouth and honor me with their lips, while their hearts are far from me." ESV

JULY 7

EVERYWHERE MATTERS

"There is no space where God is not. Yet, I can eliminate Him from the space which is me. And if He has granted me that kind of power, I should probably be far too scared to ever use it."
— Craig D. Lounsbrough

What is your definition of free will?
How has it worked for you and against you in the past?

_____
_____
_____
_____
_____
_____
_____
_____
_____
_____

1 Corinthians 6:12 "All things are lawful for me," but not all things are helpful. "All things are lawful for me," but I will not be dominated by anything." ESV

ART CHALLENGE #2

WORD ART

Utilize acrostic poetry, short stories, word cloud, etc. to represent the Chosen Life principle through word art.

CHALLENGE

Compliment yourself & others throughout the day.

ART CHALLENGE #3

MOVEMENT ART

Utilize dance, human twister poses, acting, etc. to represent the Chosen Life principle through movement art.

CHALLENGE

Try to dance like no one is watching. Be spontaneous and seize the moment.

JULY 8

EVERYWHERE MATTERS

"Stop and listen. The story is everywhere."
— Thomas Lloyd Qualls

How well do you listen? What are you doing that may be preventing you from hearing the full story? What adjustments can be made?

___

Proverbs 2:2 "Making your ear attentive to wisdom and inclining your heart to understanding." ESV

EVERYWHERE MATTERS

"Everything will not work out for you, everyone will not work out for you, every time things may not work out, every where things may not work out but some things work out, someone works out, sometime works out and some places it works out so let's be grateful for where it does work out and stop wasting time where it doesn't!" — Jaya Bhateja

How do you process successes and/or setbacks? Is this a benefit or barrier?

_____
_____
_____
_____
_____
_____
_____
_____
_____
_____

Romans 8:28 "And we know that for those who love God all things work together for good, for those who are called according to His purpose." ESV

JULY 10

EVERYWHERE MATTERS

"Biker George says you're not alone anywhere when you know The One who's with you everywhere." — Dano Janowski

Where do you draw your strength from during times of isolation? Explain how.

_____
_____
_____
_____
_____
_____
_____
_____
_____
_____
_____
_____

Psalm 23:4 "Even though I walk through the valley of the shadow of death, I will fear no evil, for you are with me." ESV

JULY 11

EVERYWHERE MATTERS

"Everywhere, I see flowers, clouds, sunshine, butterflies, songs, poems and words, of you." — Petra Hermans

Who or what puts you in a good mood?
What things represent their presence or character?

_____
_____
_____
_____
_____
_____
_____
_____
_____
_____

1 Peter 1:13 "Therefore, preparing your minds for action, and being sober-minded, set your hope fully on the grace that will be brought to you at the revelation of Jesus Christ." ESV

JULY 12

EVERYWHERE MATTERS

"Beauty is everywhere, everywhere where Nature is."
— Efrat Cybulkiewicz

What is your definition of beauty and where do you find its dwelling place?

_____
_____
_____
_____
_____
_____
_____
_____
_____
_____
_____
_____
_____

Isaiah 6:3 "Holy, holy, holy is the LORD Almighty; the whole earth is full of His glory." ESV

JULY 13

EVERYWHERE MATTERS

"Wise leaders never stop learning. They learn every day, every time and everywhere." — Gift Gugu Mona

When and where were you during the most powerful learning experiences of your life? Explain why.

_____
_____
_____
_____
_____
_____
_____
_____
_____
_____
_____
_____
_____
_____

Proverbs 1:5 "Let the wise hear and increase in learning, and the one who understands obtain guidance." ESV

JULY 14

EVERYWHERE MATTERS

"I'm everywhere, but you have to search for me. It's easy to find me. (God)" — *Kamaran Ihsan Salih*

What are you looking for to find fulfillment?
When you find it how will you know?

_____
_____
_____
_____
_____
_____
_____
_____
_____
_____
_____
_____

Proverbs 13:12 "Hope deferred makes the heart sick, but a desire fulfilled is a tree of life." ESV

JULY 15

EVERYWHERE MATTERS

"I was mistaken when I said you live in my heart. How absurd I was when you live in my fingertips so that everything I touch is you. How foolish I was when you live in my toes so that everywhere I go there's you. How senseless of me to say you live in my heart when you breathe in my lungs, walk on my mind, and drink in my mouth. I came to pen another poem for you, but even every unwritten poem is you." — Kamand Kojouri

How do you experience love? Is love about doing or being? Explain why?

_____
_____
_____
_____
_____
_____
_____

I Corinthians 13:13 "So now faith, hope, and love abide, these three; but the greatest of these is love." ESV

ART CHALLENGE #4

MUSIC ART

Utilize instrumentals, lyrics, or diverse genres to represent the Chosen Life principle through music art.

CHALLENGE

Identify the song that represents the soundtrack of your life.

ART CHALLENGE #5

CULINARY ART

Utilize cooking, baking, drink design, and the 5 senses (sight, touch, smell, taste, and hearing) to represent the Chosen Life principle through culinary art.

CHALLENGE

Create a tour of food memories where you eat a meal from each of the 7 continents.

JULY 16

EVERYWHERE MATTERS

"Until you see beauty everywhere, in every face, until then, you are blind." — Kamand Kojouri

What is your life perspective?
Are you viewing it through dirty glasses? Explain why or why not.

_____
_____
_____
_____
_____
_____
_____
_____
_____
_____

2 Corinthians 4:18 "As we look not to the things that are seen but to the things that are unseen. For the things that are seen are transient, but the things that are unseen are eternal." ESV

JULY 17

EVERYWHERE MATTERS

"A little piece of everywhere I go becomes a big part of everything I do." — Richie Norton

How have your experiences shaped your path? Describe 2-3 key moments.

_____
_____
_____
_____
_____
_____
_____
_____
_____
_____
_____

Job 12:12 "Wisdom is with the aged, and understanding in length of days." ESV

JULY 18

EVERYWHERE MATTERS

"Every day, everywhere we are surrounded by positive things, but will you choose to see them?" — Nabil N. Jamal

Are you open-minded or close-minded? Is the glass usually half full or empty? Is this pattern of thinking a benefit or barrier?

_____
_____
_____
_____
_____
_____
_____
_____
_____
_____
_____

Proverbs 1:20-21 "Wisdom cries aloud in the street, in the markets she raises her voice; at the head of the noisy streets she cries out; at the entrance of the city gates she speaks." ESV

JULY 19

EVERYWHERE MATTERS

"Tell me, about the light that you are trying to find. Tell me, where you are searching for it. For all the places you had been and for every moment you failed. You forgot to look around and realise that everyone you meet, is doing the same. The day you realise that the light, which you always searched for, was inside you. And you are the home, for all the answers to every question you ever had. The time will freeze at once for you. You become the light that you always searched." — Akshay Vasu

What does the best version of yourself look-feel-sound like?

_____
_____
_____
_____
_____
_____
_____

2 Corinthians 4:6 For God, who said, "Let light shine out of darkness," has shone in our hearts to give the light of the knowledge of the glory of God in the face of Jesus Christ." ESV

JULY 20

EVERYWHERE MATTERS

"With no name attached to it, the place somehow declared itself nowhere and everywhere at the same time" — Adam P. Knave

What are the places, people, things, and experiences that you refuse to define? Has this decision been a help or a hurt to you? Explain why or why not.

_____
_____
_____
_____
_____
_____
_____
_____
_____
_____

Romans 4:15-16 "For the law brings wrath, but where there is no law there is no transgression. That is why it depends on faith, in order that the promise may rest on grace." ESV

JULY 21

EVERYWHERE MATTERS

"Everywhere you travel to, be fully there." — *Lailah Gifty Akita*

How has your presence been a present to family, friends, coworkers, and community members?
Are you a gift to all who experience you? Explain why or why not.

_____
_____
_____
_____
_____
_____
_____
_____
_____
_____
_____

Romans 14:16-19 "So do not let what you regard as good be spoken of as evil. For the kingdom of God is not a matter of eating and drinking but of righteousness and peace and joy in the Holy Spirit. Whoever thus serves Christ is acceptable to God and approved by men. So then let us pursue what makes for peace and for mutual upbuilding." ESV

JULY 22

EVERYWHERE MATTERS

"With our instinct we can go everywhere, but with our intelligence we will get there." — Jan Jansen

How have you used instinct to fuel and energize your journey and intelligence to plot your path?

_____
_____
_____
_____
_____
_____
_____
_____
_____
_____
_____

John 14:1, 6 "Let not your hearts be troubled. Believe in God; believe also in me; Jesus said to him, "I am the way, and the truth, and the life. No one comes to the Father except through me." ESV

JULY 23

EVERYWHERE MATTERS

"Inspired moments are everywhere, regardless if we see them, seek them, or are in a space to take them in or not."
— Elaina Marie

Which moments of inspiration were born out of expectation and which came as a surprise? Explain.

_____
_____
_____
_____
_____
_____
_____
_____
_____
_____

Job 32:8 "But it is the spirit in a person, the breath of the Almighty, that makes them understand." ESV

ART CHALLENGE #6

FASHION ART

Utilize clothing, make-up, or jewelry art, interior design work, etc. to represent the Chosen Life principle through fashion art.

CHALLENGE

Buy yourself a new pair of cozy lounge wear outfits. Include a pair of sensory-friendly slippers.

ART CHALLENGE #7

SILENT ART

Utilize meditation, mindfulness and quiet time, etc. to represent the Chosen Life principle through silent art.

CHALLENGE

Go to a scenic place and sit in silence. Enjoy the experience.

JULY 24

EVERYWHERE MATTERS

"Have you been to a place where no one has been before? I give you the answer: Yes! Everywhere changes from one second to another and wherever you go, you will always be the first visitor!"
— *Mehmet Murat ildan*

Do you see yourself as a trailblazer or pioneer? Why or why not? How have you been the first to explore, evolve, or elevate?

_____
_____
_____
_____
_____
_____
_____
_____
_____

James 1:18 "Of His own will He brought us forth by the word of truth, that we should be a kind of first-fruits of His creatures." ESV

JULY 25

EVERYWHERE MATTERS

"Every idea travels to somewhere but some ideas travel to everywhere, the great ideas!"
—Mehmet Murat ildan

Describe a time when your idea(s) took off and sparked a movement or momentum? How were you and others impacted?

_____
_____
_____
_____
_____
_____
_____
_____
_____
_____

I Corinthians 9:22 "I have become all things to all people, that by all means I might save some." ESV

JULY 26

EVERYWHERE MATTERS

"Once we start to act, hope is everywhere. So instead of looking for hope, look for action. Then, and only then, hope will come."
—Greta Thunburg

What idea(s) have you yet to act on? What are you waiting for and why?

_____
_____
_____
_____
_____
_____
_____
_____
_____
_____

Proverbs 14:23 "In all toil there is profit, but mere talk tends only to poverty." ESV

JULY 27

EVERYWHERE MATTERS

"Logic will get you from A to B. Imagination will take you everywhere." –Albert Einstein

What are the benefits and barriers of logic and imagination? Which one do you value the most and prefer?

_____
_____
_____
_____
_____
_____
_____
_____
_____
_____
_____
_____

1 Corinthians 14:15 "What am I to do? I will pray with my spirit, but I will pray with my mind also; I will sing praise with my spirit, but I will sing with my mind also." ESV

JULY 28

EVERYWHERE MATTERS

"Spread love everywhere you go. Let no one ever come to you without leaving happier." –Mother Teresa

How do you ensure that people leave your presence better than when they came? Ask 3 people to share how they regularly experience you.

_____
_____
_____
_____
_____
_____
_____
_____
_____
_____
_____
_____
_____

1 Corinthians 13:4-8 "Love is patient and kind; love does not envy or boast; it is not arrogant or rude. It does not insist on its own way; it is not irritable or resentful; it does not rejoice at wrongdoing, but rejoices with the truth. Love bears all things, believes all things, hopes all things, endures all things. Love never ends." ESV

JULY 29

EVERYWHERE MATTERS

"I'm convinced of this: Good done anywhere is good done everywhere. For a change, start by speaking to people rather than walking by them like they're stones that don't matter. As long as you're breathing, it's never too late to do some good."
—Maya Angelou

What is one small habit that you have that you believe makes a huge difference? Explain.

_____
_____
_____
_____
_____
_____
_____
_____
_____
_____

Galatians 5:9 "A little leaven leavens the whole lump." ESV

JULY 30

EVERYWHERE MATTERS

"If you go looking for a friend, you're going to find they're very scarce. If you go out to be a friend, you'll find them everywhere."
—Zig Ziglar

Do you value the quality of the friendship or the quantity of friends acquired? Which is the priority and what is your role and responsibility?

_____
_____
_____
_____
_____
_____
_____
_____
_____
_____

Colossians 3:12-14 "Put on then, as God's chosen ones, holy and beloved, compassionate hearts, kindness, humility, meekness, and patience, bearing with one another and, if one has a complaint against another, forgiving each other; as the Lord has forgiven you, so you also must forgive. And above all these put on love, which binds everything together in perfect harmony." ESV

JULY 31

EVERYWHERE MATTERS

"It is possible to become discouraged about the injustice we see everywhere. But God did not promise us that the world would be humane and just. He gives us the gift of life and allows us to choose the way we will use our limited time on earth. It is an awesome opportunity." –Cesar Chavez

What part do you play in seeking and advocating for justice? How has this decision helped or caused harm? Explain.

_____
_____
_____
_____
_____
_____
_____
_____

Micah 6:8 "He (God) has told you, what is good; and what does the Lord require of you but to do justice, and to love kindness, and to walk humbly with your God." ESV

AUGUST

Key Principle #8: Never Say Never

ABSOLUTELY...STOP. GO. YIELD!!!

NEVER SAY NEVER

Trigger warning!!! This is the part of the Venn Diagram where "We" overlap. Look into the mirror. Remember the judgment that came at the cost of someone else's stumble. Now remember how quick you were to absolve yourself or dismiss your own court case when you were the one on trial? Go figure?

Taylor Swift, Michael Jordan, and Justin Bieber share the same belief. You should "Never say never." Why do "wise people" respect the "never say never" rule? But, a better question to ask is, how do these people become wise? Wisdom is an earned promotion. It comes from growing beyond knowledge and understanding through application and live demonstration. A wise person collects the lessons learned in order to uncover new strategies, refine processes, and transfer skills into new experiences.

One could infer that wisdom was gained the very moment the wise individual broke the rule/code. They failed as soon as they said it. Immediate success was experienced because they uncovered their own hypocrisy. They violated their core values or a self-promise, thus making that moment the birthplace of their newfound wisdom (i.e., lightbulb moment).

ABSOLUTELY...STOP. GO. YIELD!!!

NEVER SAY NEVER

Never is an 'absolute' word, which makes it dangerous. It has an "all-or-nothing" context and tone. Philosophers suggest that the mind can imprison us or set us free, so if you tell yourself that you will never be president, you will never try or put forth the effort. When the will set is negative so will the outcome also be. Ask yourself what are you committed to? Allow those things to refocus your mind, words, and actions.

NEVER SAY NEVER: AFFIRMATION

ME, MYSELF, & I

I will encourage myself no matter the situation or circumstance. I embrace the opportunity to be a light in dark places. I am my own accountability partner complete with wisdom and insight. I will remind myself not to judge. I admit that I have made mistakes, disappointed and/or betrayed someone or something. Therefore, I am willing to offer compassion, goodwill, and forgiveness. I should remember that, "Opportunity may only knock once but temptation definitely leans on the doorbell." Problem solving should be my immediate priority and addressed with tact, persistence, and self-esteem.

WE

We will encourage one another, others, and ourselves no matter the situation or circumstance. We embrace the opportunity to be a light in dark places. We are accountability partners complete with wisdom and insight. We will remind each other not to judge. We admit that we have made mistakes, disappointed, and/or betrayed someone or something. Therefore, we are willing to offer compassion, goodwill, and forgiveness. We should remember that, "Opportunity may only knock once but temptation definitely leans on the doorbell." Problem solving should be an immediate priority and addressed with tact, persistence, and teamwork.

ART CHALLENGE #1

VISUAL ART

Utilize photography, painting, digital media, sketching, sculpture, collage, crafts, etc. to represent the Chosen Life principle through visual art.

CHALLENGE

Create an image that represents you doing something positive that is out-of-the-box.

AUGUST 1

NEVER SAY NEVER

"You don't know what you're going to do in a situation until faced with it. Life lesson learned. I was going to have to banish 'never' from my repertoire." — Abigail Barnette

Have you ever considered banishing the word never from your speech? Why or why not? Would this choice cause harm or help you grow?

_____
_____
_____
_____
_____
_____
_____
_____
_____
_____

Matthew 7:1-2 "Judge not, that you be not judged. For with the judgment you pronounce you will be judged, and with the measure you use it will be measured to you.." ESV

AUGUST 2

NEVER SAY NEVER

"Never say never or it becomes a vice, and there you have it, you just did it twice." — Ana Claudia Antunes

Is it impossible to live a life of never? Do you believe it is a contradiction to 'never say never' because you are guilty of it before you even begin? Why or why not?

_____
_____
_____
_____
_____
_____
_____
_____
_____
_____
_____
_____
_____
_____

Romans 3:23 "For all have sinned and fall short of the glory of God." ESV

AUGUST 3

NEVER SAY NEVER

"We often betray our arrogance or immaturity by asserting that we will never do something bad that we are capable of doing."
— *Mokokoma Mokhonoana*

Is believing that you will never do something bad or convincing yourself that you are not even capable, a sign of immaturity and arrogance?
Is this belief system helpful or harmful?

_____
_____
_____
_____
_____
_____
_____
_____
_____
_____

Ecclesiastes 7:20 "Surely there is not a righteous man on earth who does good and never sins." ESV

AUGUST 4

NEVER SAY NEVER

"Don't say "never" say "not yet." Some of the most amazing things in life happen unexpectedly." — Brittany Burgunder

Can you say never without believing that it is an absolute truth? What happens if your truth is not the divine truth? Universal truth? Why or why not?

_____
_____
_____
_____
_____
_____
_____
_____
_____
_____
_____
_____

1 John 1:8 "If we say we have no sin, we deceive ourselves, and the truth is not in us." ESV

AUGUST 5

NEVER SAY NEVER

"I don't have a development deal, but the one thing I have learned is never say never. I will consider things as they come."
–Nina Garcia

What was the last 5 things that you have considered that were outside of your normal (i.e. comfort zone)? What made you open to the possibilities?

_____
_____
_____
_____
_____
_____
_____
_____
_____
_____

Isaiah 43:19 "Behold, I am doing a new thing; now it springs forth, do you not perceive it? I will make a way in the wilderness and rivers in the desert." ESV

AUGUST 6

NEVER SAY NEVER

"You never know what's going to happen. My mother was an English teacher. If someone had told her that I was going to write a book, she would never have believed that. So you can never say never." –Tony Dungy

Who are 2-3 people in your life that would be surprised that you accomplished something unthinkable? Why is this accomplishment outside of their vision of who you are or what you could accomplish?

_____
_____
_____
_____
_____
_____
_____
_____
_____
_____

Psalm 27:10 "For my father and my mother have forsaken me, but the Lord will take me in." ESV

AUGUST 7

NEVER SAY NEVER

"One day, you might look up and see me playing the game at 50. Don't laugh. Never say never, because limits, like fears, are often just an illusion." –Michael Jordan

Are the limits you believe you have just an illusion or reality? Is the fear you encounter reality or an illusion? Why or why not?

_____
_____
_____
_____
_____
_____
_____
_____
_____
_____

Mark 10:27 "Jesus looked at them and said, "With man it is impossible, but not with God. For all things are possible with God." ESV

ART CHALLENGE #2

WORD ART

Utilize acrostic poetry, short stories, word cloud, etc. to represent the Chosen Life principle through word art.

CHALLENGE

Make a list of 5 counter responses to the 5 negative self-talk thoughts that you desire to change.

ART CHALLENGE #3

MOVEMENT ART

Utilize dance, human twister poses, acting, etc. to represent the Chosen Life principle through movement art.

CHALLENGE

Strike a pose, or create a hand gesture that represents, Never Say Never.

AUGUST 8

NEVER SAY NEVER

"One thing I've learned: you never know where life is taking you, but it's taking you." — Hilary Swank

Is your life taking you places or are you in the driver's seat? Who is in control and what things are influencing you to make decisions? Are there any benefits or barriers? Why or why not?

_____
_____
_____
_____
_____
_____
_____
_____
_____
_____
_____
_____

Proverbs 16:9 "The heart of a person plans his way, but the Lord establishes their steps." ESV

AUGUST 9

NEVER SAY NEVER

"The things I never say never get me into trouble."
~ Calvin Coolidge

Are your words powerful? Do the things you say come true? Why or why not? Name 10 things that you said but wished you could erase them. Name 10 positive things that you spoke into existence.

_____
_____
_____
_____
_____
_____
_____
_____
_____
_____

Psalm 141:3 "Set a guard, O Lord, over my mouth; keep watch over the door of my lips!" ESV

NEVER SAY NEVER

"I'm telling you, people. Every day we wake up is another blessing. Follow your dreams and don't let anyone stop you. Never say never." ~ Justin Bieber

What purpose do you serve for waking up this morning? What are you assigned to do, say, or enhance? Do you consider yourself the answers to a problem only you can solve? Why or why not?

_____
_____
_____
_____
_____
_____
_____
_____
_____
_____
_____

Lamentations 3:22-23 "The steadfast love of the Lord never ceases; His mercies never come to an end; they are new every morning; great is your faithfulness." ESV

AUGUST 11

NEVER SAY NEVER

"Never say never! Never is a long, undependable time, and life is too full of rich possibilities to have restrictions placed upon it."
~ Gloria Swanson

Do you place restrictions on yourself? How has this impacted you? Name 3 restrictions you place on yourself and the possible consequences and/or celebrations? Have these 3 things helped or caused harm?

_____
_____
_____
_____
_____
_____
_____
_____
_____

Proverbs 3:1-2 "Do not forget my teaching, but let your heart keep my commandments, for length of days and years of life and peace they will add to you." ESV

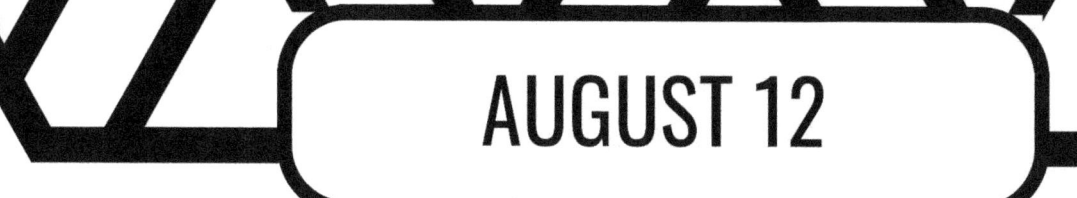

AUGUST 12

NEVER SAY NEVER

"Never say "never" about anything, because if you do, life has a way of humbling you." ~ Mike Colter

What is your definition of humble? Does a humble person refrain from subscribing to concrete thoughts or following strict behavioral boundaries? Why or why not? How would a humble person admit to changing their mind or to admitting that they were wrong?

_____
_____
_____
_____
_____
_____
_____
_____
_____
_____
_____

James 4:10 "Humble yourselves before the Lord, and He will exalt you." ESV

AUGUST 13

NEVER SAY NEVER

"Never say never, for if you live long enough, chances are you will not be able to abide by the simplest of such injunctions."
~ Gloria Swanson

How often do you change your mind? What typically motivates the shift?

___

1 Kings 3:14 "And if you will walk in my ways, keeping my statutes and my commandments...then I will lengthen your days." ESV

AUGUST 14

NEVER SAY NEVER

"Never say never. The things that you don't plan are the best. I'm a very spontaneous person." ~ Lindsay Lohan

How do you balance planning and spontaneity? Have you found the process contentious or harmonious?

_____
_____
_____
_____
_____
_____
_____
_____
_____
_____
_____

Proverbs 19:21 "Many are the plans in the mind of a man, but it is the purpose of the Lord that will stand." ESV

AUGUST 15

NEVER SAY NEVER

"I never say 'never,' and I never say 'always.'" ~ *Grace Kelly*

Is 'always' a word that you use often? Why or why not?

_____
_____
_____
_____
_____
_____
_____
_____
_____
_____
_____

Matthew 12:37 "For by your words you will be justified, and by your words you will be condemned." ESV

ART CHALLENGE #4

MUSIC ART

Utilize instrumentals, lyrics, or diverse genres to represent the Chosen Life principle through music art.

CHALLENGE

Create a jingle that will help you remember to "Never Say Never."

ART CHALLENGE #5

CULINARY ART

Utilize cooking, baking, drink design, and the 5 senses (sight, touch, smell, taste, and hearing) to represent the Chosen Life principle through culinary art.

CHALLENGE

Allow a friend to help you explore eating, smelling, or touching an exotic dish, animal, or meal.

AUGUST 16

NEVER SAY NEVER

"Let us die young, or let us live forever, We don't have the power but we Never say Never.. Sooner or later we all will be gone, why don't you stay young?" ~ Harry Styles

How does what we say impact our relevance?
Does what we do influence the magnitude of our legacy?

_____
_____
_____
_____
_____
_____
_____
_____
_____
_____

1 John 2:25 "And this is the promise that He made to us—eternal life." ESV

AUGUST 17

NEVER SAY NEVER

"It may not have the virtuous ring of the golden rule, but the maxim "never say never" is one of the most important in ethics."
~Julian Baggini

Describe a time when your 'never' became a 'now' reality. How did you respond? What did you learn about yourself from the experience?

_____
_____
_____
_____
_____
_____
_____
_____
_____
_____

Ephesians 4:29 "Let no corrupting talk come out of your mouths, but only such as is good for building up, as fits the occasion, that it may give grace to those who hear." ESV

AUGUST 18

NEVER SAY NEVER

"I try to stay friends with everybody because you might go back and work with somebody who you had a horrible experience with and it could be great the next time. You never know which way it's going to go, never say never." ~ Rob Zombie

What have your relationships taught you about valuing people vs. managing expectations? Who are 3-5 friends that have been instrumental in your growth and development?

_____
_____
_____
_____
_____
_____
_____
_____
_____
_____

Titus 3:3 "For we ourselves were once foolish, disobedient, led astray, slaves to various passions and pleasures, passing our days in malice and envy, hated by others and hating one another." ESV

AUGUST 19

NEVER SAY NEVER

"Never say never – you don't know what's going to happen in the future." ~ Nikki Sanderson

What feelings do you experience when contemplating your future? What are your intrusive thoughts? How do you manage your emotions?

_____
_____
_____
_____
_____
_____
_____
_____
_____
_____

James 4:14 "You do not know what tomorrow will bring. What is your life?" ESV

AUGUST 20

NEVER SAY NEVER

"This is a shining example of never quit, never give up, & never say never. I proved everyone wrong." ~ Mickie James

What motivates you to keep going during tough times?
What strategies or tools do you use to keep you focused?
What principles or values help you to remain grounded?

_____
_____
_____
_____
_____
_____
_____
_____
_____
_____
_____

1 Corinthians 15:58 "Therefore, my beloved, be steadfast, immovable, always abounding in the work of the Lord, knowing that in the Lord your labor is not in vain." ESV

AUGUST 21

NEVER SAY NEVER

"I'm old enough to never say never. I never had a grand plan with what I was going to do. There are some movies that I would like to be involved with, but I'm trying to be a working actor." ~ Dennis Farina

What dreams and desires are still in your heart to accomplish? Why do you want to see them happen? What have you done to bring them to fruition?

_____
_____
_____
_____
_____
_____
_____
_____
_____
_____

Proverbs 3:5-6 "Trust in the Lord with all your heart, and do not lean on your own understanding. In all your ways acknowledge Him, and He will make straight your paths." ESV

AUGUST 22

NEVER SAY NEVER

"Cowards die many times before their deaths; the valiant never taste of death but once." ~William Shakespeare

What dream(s) has fear killed inside of you?
What dream(s) has your courage brought to life?
What have you learned about yourself through your fear and courage?

_____
_____
_____
_____
_____
_____
_____
_____
_____
_____
_____

Proverbs 18:21 "Death and life are in the power of the tongue, and those who love it will eat its fruits." ESV

AUGUST 23

NEVER SAY NEVER

"Listen to the mustn't, child. Listen to the don'ts. Listen to the shouldn't, the impossible, the won't. Listen to the never haves, then listen close to me... Anything can happen, child. Anything can be."
~Shel Silverstein

How many times a day do you hear don't, shouldn't and can't? When was the last time you replaced a mustn't, don't, shouldn't or won't with the 'anything can happen' mentality? How did this mindset change the outcome?

_____
_____
_____
_____
_____
_____
_____
_____
_____

Luke 8:15 "As for that in the good soil, they are those who, hearing the word, hold it fast in an honest and good heart, and bear fruit with patience." ESV

ART CHALLENGE #6

FASHION ART

Utilize clothing, make-up, or jewelry art, interior design work, etc. to represent the Chosen Life principle through fashion art.

CHALLENGE

Boldly wear the color that you tell yourself you don't look good wearing.

ART CHALLENGE #7

SILENT ART

Utilize meditation, mindfulness, and quiet time, etc. to represent the Chosen Life principle through silent art.

CHALLENGE

Meditate on how you would recover if you violated one of your values. Visualize how your mistakes can be used to motivate others.

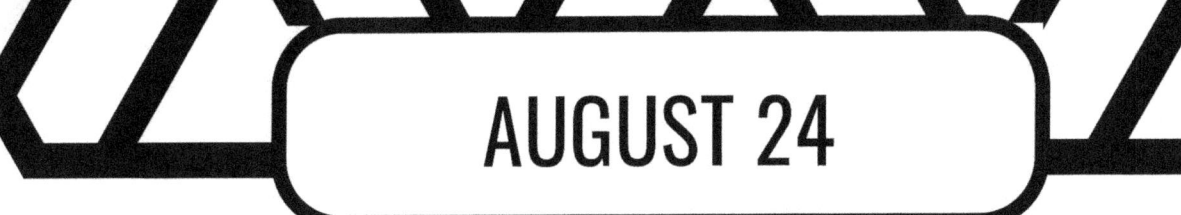

AUGUST 24

NEVER SAY NEVER

"Never put off till tomorrow what may be done the day after tomorrow just as well." –Mark Twain

How do you prioritize what matters most today? How do you determine what to do and when you will get it done? Think about your formula and assess if it is solid or needs work? Measure your effectiveness by your ability to get things done.

_____
_____
_____
_____
_____
_____
_____
_____
_____
_____

Hebrews 3:13 "But exhort one another every day, as long as it is called "today," that none of you may be hardened by the deceitfulness of sin." ESV

NEVER SAY NEVER

"A woman is like a tea bag; you never know how strong it is until it's in hot water." ~Eleanor Roosevelt

Do you consider yourself to be 'strong?' Why or why not?
When do you demonstrate this characteristic most?
When you are in hot water or when the waters are calm and cold?

_____
_____
_____
_____
_____
_____
_____
_____
_____
_____
_____
_____

Nahum 1:7 "The Lord is good, a stronghold in the day of trouble; He knows those who take refuge in Him." ESV

AUGUST 26

NEVER SAY NEVER

"I've learned that people will forget what you said, people will forget what you did, but people will never forget how you made them feel." ~Maya Angelou

Why are feelings long-lasting? Why do we remember a person who offended us as far back in elementary school?
In what ways do you manage how you treat people in order not to offend?

_____
_____
_____
_____
_____
_____
_____
_____
_____
_____

1 Thessalonians 5:11 "Therefore encourage one another and build one another up, just as you are doing." ESV

AUGUST 27

NEVER SAY NEVER

"Tired, tired with nothing, tired with everything, tired with the world's weight he had never chosen to bear."
— F. Scott Fitzgerald

Are you tired from the pressures of life? Are you restless when things are calm and too quiet? Are you stressed when things are too noisy and fast moving? When are you ever at peace and full of energy?

_____
_____
_____
_____
_____
_____
_____
_____
_____
_____

Isaiah 40:31 "But they who wait for the Lord shall renew their strength; they shall mount up with wings like eagles; they shall run and not be weary; they shall walk and not faint." ESV

AUGUST 28

NEVER SAY NEVER

"Never fall in love?" "Always," said the count. "I am always in love." — Ernest Hemingway

Think of the 10 best acts or deeds that you have done throughout your life. Were they done in love of self or service to others? Were they motivated out of obedience and loyalty to a power bigger than yourself?

_____
_____
_____
_____
_____
_____
_____
_____
_____
_____
_____

1 Corinthians 16:14 "Let all that you do be done in love." ESV

AUGUST 29

NEVER SAY NEVER

"If bees die, people will die. Only ignorance never dies! ("Why step out of nature?")" — Erik Pevernagie

Do you believe that intelligence will outlive ignorance or vice versa? Which would die first if you had to make a choice and why? What evidence from the way we live and behave bring you to this conclusion?

_____
_____
_____
_____
_____
_____
_____
_____
_____
_____

Hosea 4:6 "My people are destroyed for lack of knowledge; And since you have forgotten the law of your God, I also will forget your children." ESV

AUGUST 30

NEVER SAY NEVER

"For the first time in my life I understood the meaning of the word 'never'. And it's really awful. You say the word a hundred times a day but you don't really know what you're saying until you're faced with a real 'never again'." — Muriel Barbery

When has the expression 'never again' come to life for you (i.e. funeral)? How did it impact you and your loved ones?

_____
_____
_____
_____
_____
_____
_____
_____
_____
_____
_____

Psalm 19:14 "Let the words of my mouth and the meditation of my heart be acceptable in your sight, O Lord, my rock and my redeemer." ESV

AUGUST 31

NEVER SAY NEVER

"There's never an easy route to the things that matter."
— Charles de Lint

How challenging has the route been towards getting to where you intend to go? Describe the peaks and valleys along the way.
Have these experiences helped to sharpen your skill set or will set?

_____
_____
_____
_____
_____
_____
_____
_____
_____
_____

Matthew 7:13-14 "Enter by the narrow gate. For the gate is wide and the way is easy that leads to destruction, and those who enter by it are many. For the gate is narrow and the way is hard that leads to life, and those who find it are few." ESV

SEPTEMBER

Key Principle #9: Living Not Existing

THE BEST LIFE... IS AN ARTFUL ONE!

LIVING NOT EXISTING

When did you experience your first "hamster wheel" moment? Was it after a vacation? Did it occur following a discussion with a friend? Perhaps it was during a TV series binge. Regardless of the scenario, it can be a disheartening moment.

The idea that your hard work and time may not result in the ROI (return on investment) you expect is compounded even further when you consider that your blood, sweat, and years may actually be contributing to the advancement and stability of others.

In your defense, no one ever plans to run full speed in place (unless you're on a treadmill). However, after obtaining the job, getting the car, securing the home, something interesting happened. Instead of those things honoring their position as your servants, you begin to live in service to them. More work for more money for more bills and more repairs. The faster you run, the more exhausted you become. Sound familiar?

If you think this is the part where we suggest giving up your quality of life to "live free" - think again! This is more about challenging you to be honest with yourself about what fulfills you.

THE BEST LIFE... IS AN ARTFUL ONE!

LIVING NOT EXISTING

What charges your batteries? What undertakings challenge you in ways that build your skillset? What things interest you? What are your passions? There are more sides and layers to you than you care to admit.

Stop ignoring them! The goal is not just to get off the hamster wheel, but to leap out of the cage. You were never meant to spend all of that energy to remain stationary. Move! Live! Be!

LIVING NOT EXISTING: AFFIRMATION

ME, MYSELF & I

I will breathe, let go, and remind myself that this moment is the only one we have for certain. I will live the life of my dreams and balance my work and play time. I will make strategic adjustments to each so that work feels like play and play begins to fuel my work. This approach will help prevent work from becoming a weekly overload recreational killer (w.o.r.k.) and lead to a balanced relationship with self and others.

WE

We will breathe, let go, and remind ourselves that this moment is the only one we have for certain. We will live the life of our dreams and balance our work and play time. We will make strategic adjustments to each so that work feels like play and play begins to fuel our work. This approach will help prevent work from becoming a weekly overload recreational killer (w.o.r.k.) and lead to balanced relationships.

ART CHALLENGE #1

VISUAL ART

Utilize photography, painting, digital media, sketching, sculpture, collage, crafts, etc. to represent the Chosen Life principle through visual art.

CHALLENGE

Create a vision board that reflects your thriving life in the next 1-5 years.

SEPTEMBER 1

LIVING NOT EXISTING

"Learn to light a candle in the darkest moments of someone's life. Be the light that helps others see; it is what gives life its deepest significance." — *Roy T. Bennett*

When was the last time that you were able to be the light for someone dealing with a dark situation? What was your strategy and why?

_____
_____
_____
_____
_____
_____
_____
_____
_____
_____

John 8:12 "I am the light of the world. Whoever follows me will not walk in darkness, but will have the light of life." ESV

SEPTEMBER 2

LIVING NOT EXISTING

"To live, to TRULY live, we must be willing to RISK. To be nothing in order to find everything. To leap before we look."
— *Mandy Hale*

Are you a risk-taker? Is your life more fulfilled or more depleted? Name 3 areas of your life where you would like to take more risk. What is your first step in that direction?

_____
_____
_____
_____
_____
_____
_____
_____
_____
_____

Acts 14:22 "Strengthening the souls of the disciples, encouraging them to continue in the faith, and saying that through many tribulations we must enter the kingdom of God." ESV

SEPTEMBER 3

LIVING NOT EXISTING

"Reading the Bible will help you get to know the word, but it's when you put it down and live your life that you get to know the author." — Steve Maraboli

How well are you doing at applying what you are learning? Are you more satisfied with knowledge that you avoid action?
What are your opportunities for growth in this area?

_____
_____
_____
_____
_____
_____
_____
_____
_____
_____

Psalm 25:14 "The friendship of the Lord is for those who fear Him, and He makes known to them His covenant." ESV

SEPTEMBER 4

LIVING NOT EXISTING

"Make your lives a masterpiece, you only get one canvas."
— E.A. Bucchianeri

Are you living or merely existing? Do you have purpose and vision for your career, family, and personal interests? Why or why not?

James 4:14 "Yet you do not know what tomorrow will bring. What is your life? For you are a mist that appears for a little time and then vanishes." ESV

SEPTEMBER 5

LIVING NOT EXISTING

"Live full, die empty" — *Les Brown*

What does it mean to live a full life? Name 2-3 people that lived a full life and explain why you believe they died empty? Was this a good or bad thing?

_____
_____
_____
_____
_____
_____
_____
_____
_____
_____
_____
_____

2 Timothy 4:7 "I have fought the good fight, I have finished the race, I have kept the faith." ESV

SEPTEMBER 6

LIVING NOT EXISTING

"You can't do passion halfway. Living your passion means you're all in. You trust your heart and trust your gut wherever that takes you." — Joe Plumeri

What are you passionate about and why? Have you ever run low on the fuel (i.e. energy) that is required to keep your passion projects alive? Why or why not? What were the learned lessons?

_____
_____
_____
_____
_____
_____
_____
_____
_____
_____
_____
_____

Romans 12:11 "Do not be slothful in zeal, be fervent in spirit, serve the Lord." ESV

SEPTEMBER 7

LIVING NOT EXISTING

"Be brave and take risks... You don't have to have it all figured out to move forward." — Roy Bennett

How do you approach moving forward? Do you struggle without having all of the answers? What do you rely on or focus on? What are the patterns of behavior that prevent you from moving forward?

_____
_____
_____
_____
_____
_____
_____
_____
_____
_____

Joshua 1:9 "Have I not commanded you? Be strong and courageous. Do not be frightened, and do not be dismayed, for the Lord your God is with you wherever you go." ESV

ART CHALLENGE #2

WORD ART

Utilize acrostic poetry, short stories, word cloud, etc. to represent the Chosen Life principle through word art.

CHALLENGE

Set your phone reminders with uplifting words.

ART CHALLENGE #3

MOVEMENT ART

Utilize dance, human twister poses, acting, etc. to represent the Chosen Life principle through movement art.

CHALLENGE

Act out the scene in your personal life movie when you accomplish your biggest dream.

SEPTEMBER 8

LIVING NOT EXISTING

"Are you living fully, loving completely, learning constantly, and planning to leave a worthwhile legacy?" — Steve Goodier

How do you desire to be loved? Do you give what you expect to get? What do you want your legacy to be regardless of how others treat you?

_____
_____
_____
_____
_____
_____
_____
_____
_____
_____
_____
_____

Psalm 145:4 "One generation shall commend your works to another, and shall declare your mighty acts." ESV

SEPTEMBER 9

LIVING NOT EXISTING

"Look around you. A fear of living, of truly living, is the most common fear there is." — T.M Cicinski

Does fear rule your life? If so, in which areas (i.e. career, family, hobbies, etc.,)? How do you prevent fear from taking over? What are your strategies?

_____
_____
_____
_____
_____
_____
_____
_____
_____
_____

John 10:10 "The thief comes only to steal and kill and destroy. I came that they may have life and have it abundantly." ESV

SEPTEMBER 10

LIVING NOT EXISTING

"If you want to be happy, do not dwell in the past, do not worry about the future, focus on living fully in the present."
— Roy T. Bennett

Do you focus more on the past, present, or future? Which dimension makes you happiest? If the present time period doesn't bring as much joy, how can you focus more on the positive?

_____
_____
_____
_____
_____
_____
_____
_____
_____
_____

Philippians 3:13-14 "But one thing I do, forgetting those things which are behind and reaching forward to those things which are ahead, I press toward the goal for the prize of the upward call of God in Christ Jesus." ESV

SEPTEMBER 11

LIVING NOT EXISTING

"Life requires a childlike approach to grasp what a miracle it is to just live." — Richelle E. Goodrich

Is your approach to live life childlike? How can you reset your adult mindset to get back to the freedom and genuine joy experienced during the happiest moment of childhood?

_____
_____
_____
_____
_____
_____
_____
_____
_____
_____

Matthew 18:3 "Truly, I say to you, unless you turn and become like children, you will never enter the kingdom of heaven." ESV

SEPTEMBER 12

LIVING NOT EXISTING

"Life is all about survival, life is living, and life is reaching the end" — Josephs Quartzy

Are you living your life with the end goal in mind? Are you surviving and thriving in the areas of your destiny? If not, what are you willing to start, stop, and continue doing?

_____
_____
_____
_____
_____
_____
_____
_____
_____
_____
_____
_____

Matthew 24:13 "But the one who endures to the end will be saved." ESV

SEPTEMBER 13

LIVING NOT EXISTING

"Living your life without knowing your worth is a sin."
— *Nitin Namdeo*

Do you know your worth?
What is connected to and how do you share/reflect this with/to others?

_____
_____
_____
_____
_____
_____
_____
_____
_____
_____

Psalm 139:23-24 "Search me, O God, and know my heart! Try me and know my thoughts! And see if there be any grievous way in me, and lead me in the way everlasting!" ESV

SEPTEMBER 14

LIVING NOT EXISTING

"The surest way to make your dreams come true is to live them."
— *Roy T. Bennett*

Are you living your dreams out loud? Why or why not?
What are your dreams and how are they evolving?
What are they requiring you to start, stop, and continue doing?

_____
_____
_____
_____
_____
_____
_____
_____
_____
_____
_____

Proverbs 21:21 "Whoever pursues righteousness and kindness will find life, righteousness, and honor." ESV

SEPTEMBER 15

LIVING NOT EXISTING

"Life is a great puzzle that is woven into the pieces of time. The more we live the more apparent it gets, and it makes more sense"
— *Dr. Lucas D. Shallua*

How do the pieces of your life paint a big picture? What does it look like? What is the message and meaning?

_____
_____
_____
_____
_____
_____
_____
_____
_____
_____

Ephesians 5:15-16 "Look carefully then how you walk, not as unwise but as wise, making the best use of the time, because the days are evil." ESV

ART CHALLENGE #4

MUSIC ART

Utilize instrumentals, lyrics, or diverse genres to represent the Chosen Life principle through music art.

CHALLENGE

Identify a song that gives you life. A musical experience that energizes the soul.

ART CHALLENGE #5

CULINARY ART

Utilize cooking, baking, drink design, and the 5 senses (sight, touch, smell, taste, and hearing) to represent the Chosen Life principle through culinary art.

CHALLENGE

Eat 3 meals that only include foods that reflect life (i.e., Salads, fruits, vegetables, etc.). No dead items.

SEPTEMBER 16

LIVING NOT EXISTING

"Life is a school of learning, the more learning you make, the better living will be." — Pawan Pandit

What are the last 3-5 things that you have recently learned? Would you like to have a happy life? Does this require learning and growing?

___

Proverbs 1:5 "Let the wise hear and increase in learning, and the one who understands obtain guidance." ESV

SEPTEMBER 17

LIVING NOT EXISTING

"My attitude jump starts the energy I am living in!"
— *Allan Rufus*

How would you describe your attitude? Does it align with the energy you need? Does your attitude control your energy or does your energy control your attitude?

_____
_____
_____
_____
_____
_____
_____
_____
_____
_____

Colossians 1:29 "For this I toil, struggling with all His energy that He powerfully works within me." ESV

SEPTEMBER 18

LIVING NOT EXISTING

"Let the improvement of yourself keep you so busy that you have no time to criticize others." — Roy Bennett

Which areas of life are you satisfied with and which do you desire to be improved? Why or why not? What should you start, stop, and continue doing?

_____
_____
_____
_____
_____
_____
_____
_____
_____
_____
_____

Matthew 7:1-2 "Judge not, that you be not judged. For with the judgment you pronounce you will be judged, and with the measure you use it will be measured to you." ESV

SEPTEMBER 19

LIVING NOT EXISTING

"Our life is full of additions and multiplications. If you are not afraid of subtractions and divisions, you are on the way to attain salvation!" — Abhijit Kar Gupta

How do you embrace the additions and subtractions inflicted by life? What are your emotional responses to life, death, new beginnings and changes? What strategies work to help and which hurt?

_____
_____
_____
_____
_____
_____
_____
_____

Psalm 16:11 You make known to me the path of life; in your presence there is fullness of joy; at your right hand are pleasures forevermore.

SEPTEMBER 20

LIVING NOT EXISTING

"If you know how quickly people forget the dead you will start living your life on your own terms instead of other people's terms." — Samuel Clément

Are you afraid of being forgotten? Are the opinions of others guiding your life, choices, and thoughts? Why or why not?

_____
_____
_____
_____
_____
_____
_____
_____
_____
_____

Luke 9:60 "Let the dead bury their own dead. But as for you, go and proclaim the kingdom of God." ESV

SEPTEMBER 21

LIVING NOT EXISTING

"No amount of regretting can change the past, and no amount of worrying can change the future." — Roy T. Bennett

Are you consumed with regret and worry? If so, why? If not how do you prevent yourself from worrying and regret? What does this look-feel-sound like?

_____
_____
_____
_____
_____
_____
_____
_____
_____
_____

Ephesians 1:10 "As a plan for the fullness of time, to unite all things in Him, things in heaven and things on earth." ESV

SEPTEMBER 22

LIVING NOT EXISTING

"All art stems from an irrepressible urge to share emotion. The best artists have lived; and, in that living, endured profound heartache and blissful joy." — Wayne Gerard Trotman

Which areas of art attract you the most? Why?
How does it help, heal, or bring harmony to your life?

_____
_____
_____
_____
_____
_____
_____
_____
_____
_____

Romans 12:6 "Having gifts that differ according to the grace given to us, let us use them." ESV

SEPTEMBER 23

LIVING NOT EXISTING

"Yeah, but just being alive doesn't mean all that much on its own. How you live is more important." — Genki Kawamura

Are you satisfied with how you are living?
How would you encourage a friend to not be satisfied with just existing by living on purpose, moving toward their destiny?

_____
_____
_____
_____
_____
_____
_____
_____
_____
_____

Psalm 121:7-8 "The Lord will keep you from all evil; He will keep your life. The Lord will keep your going out and your coming in from this time forth and forevermore." ESV

ART CHALLENGE #6

FASHION ART

Utilize clothing, make-up, or jewelry art, interior design work, etc. to represent the Chosen Life principle through fashion art.

CHALLENGE

Pose for a picture dressed in the fashion look that represents living your best life.

ART CHALLENGE #7

SILENT ART

Utilize meditation, mindfulness, and quiet time, etc. to represent the Chosen Life principle through silent art.

CHALLENGE

Visualize the best way to pamper yourself. Meditate on the mood that will be the end reward.

SEPTEMBER 24

LIVING NOT EXISTING

"Most live the life whining, some live it weeping and few live it laughing." — Amit Kalantri

When was the last time you laughed uncontrollably? How do you keep yourself from whining and weeping? What are some reasons that you may begin to whine or weep? How do you recover? Why or why not?

_____
_____
_____
_____
_____
_____
_____
_____
_____
_____
_____

Proverbs 17:22 "A merry heart does good, like medicine, but a broken spirit dries the bones." ESV

SEPTEMBER 25

LIVING NOT EXISTING

"Life is a slideshow of stories that we create with each passing moment. Let each slide be Worth It!" — Live Life

Why/How is the story of your life worth sharing? What additional scenes would you create if you had no limits or restrictions?

_____
_____
_____
_____
_____
_____
_____
_____
_____
_____

Isaiah 41:10 "Fear not, for I am with you; be not dismayed, for I am your God; I will strengthen you, I will help you, I will uphold you with my righteous right hand." ESV

SEPTEMBER 26

LIVING NOT EXISTING

"To live with hope is to seek heavenly help."
— Lailah Gifty Akita

What does hope look-feel-sound like to you? Is it easy to accomplish by human effort or is it accomplished only through existential help?

_____
_____
_____
_____
_____
_____
_____
_____
_____
_____

Romans 15:13 "May the God of hope fill you with all joy and peace in believing, so that by the power of the Holy Spirit you may abound in hope." ESV

SEPTEMBER 27

LIVING NOT EXISTING

"It is nothing to die. It is frightful not to live."
— *Victor Hugo*

Why is it easier to give up but scary to live with intention and purpose? What are the benefits and barriers of each?

_____
_____
_____
_____
_____
_____
_____
_____
_____
_____
_____
_____

Philippians 1:21 "For to me to live is Christ, and to die is gain." ESV

SEPTEMBER 28

LIVING NOT EXISTING

"In life one has a choice to take one of two paths: to wait for some special day – or to celebrate each special day."
— Rasheed Ogunlaru

Which is easier for you, to wait for a special day or to make every day special? What is your strategy or struggle? Is making every day special authentic to who you are (i.e. organic) or a full time job?

_____
_____
_____
_____
_____
_____
_____
_____
_____
_____

Matthew 7:13-14 "Enter by the narrow gate. For the gate is wide and the way is easy that leads to destruction, and those who enter by it are many. For the gate is narrow and the way is hard that leads to life, and those who find it are few." ESV

SEPTEMBER 29

LIVING NOT EXISTING

"The question isn't "Why do we die?" The question is "Why do we live?"" — S.M. Reine

Do you know and understand the purpose of your life? How does what you do and how you show up in your relationships align with your life's purpose?

_____
_____
_____
_____
_____
_____
_____
_____
_____
_____

Romans 11:36 "For everything comes from Him and exists by His power and is intended for His glory. All glory to Him forever!" ESV

SEPTEMBER 30

LIVING NOT EXISTING

"Quit planning your dream and start living it." — Alan Cohen

Are you a planner? Does this prevent you from being a doer? What steps do you need to employ in order to make your dreams come true?

_____
_____
_____
_____
_____
_____
_____
_____
_____
_____
_____
_____

James 2:26 "For as the body apart from the spirit is dead, so also faith apart from works is dead." ESV

OCTOBER

Key Principle #10: Inside Out Before Outside In

CHARACTER VS. PHYSICAL TRAITS

INSIDE OUT BEFORE OUTSIDE IN

Pop Quiz!!! Would you rather be intelligent or attractive? Would you rather be strong in character traits or strong in physical traits? Why do we put ourselves in boxes? We get extremely upset when others force us to fit into their tiny stereotypical boxes, but gladly participate in games like, "Would You Rather."

Perhaps, one good quality of the game is that it forces us to prioritize what matters most. We internally wrestle with the thoughts... *What do I prioritize, the internal and the external factors in life?* Can I really possess both?

Yes. The two can coexist: intelligence and attraction and strong character and physical traits. Being your authentic self sounds good, but how do you accomplish this if you are uncertain? Ask a close friend how they experience you when things are great and when you are stressed? Do you speak, behave, or act differently when you are around different social groups?

MASK alert!!! You might be wearing a hypothetical mask. We should each audit how we are engaging with our friends, family, community, and loved ones. If you are wearing a mask in certain environments, then focus on internal self-awareness. Masks Off today!!!

INSIDE OUT BEFORE OUTSIDE IN: AFFIRMATION

ME, MYSELF, & I

I am painting my own canvas thought-by-thought, choice-by-choice, through every experience. I will commit to mirror work, self-reflection, self-assessment, and effective responses. My final masterpiece will showcase the fruit of my labor.

WE

We are painting our own canvas thought-by-thought, choice-by-choice, through every experience. We will commit to mirror work, self-reflection, self-assessment, and effective responses. Our final masterpiece will showcase the fruit of our labor.

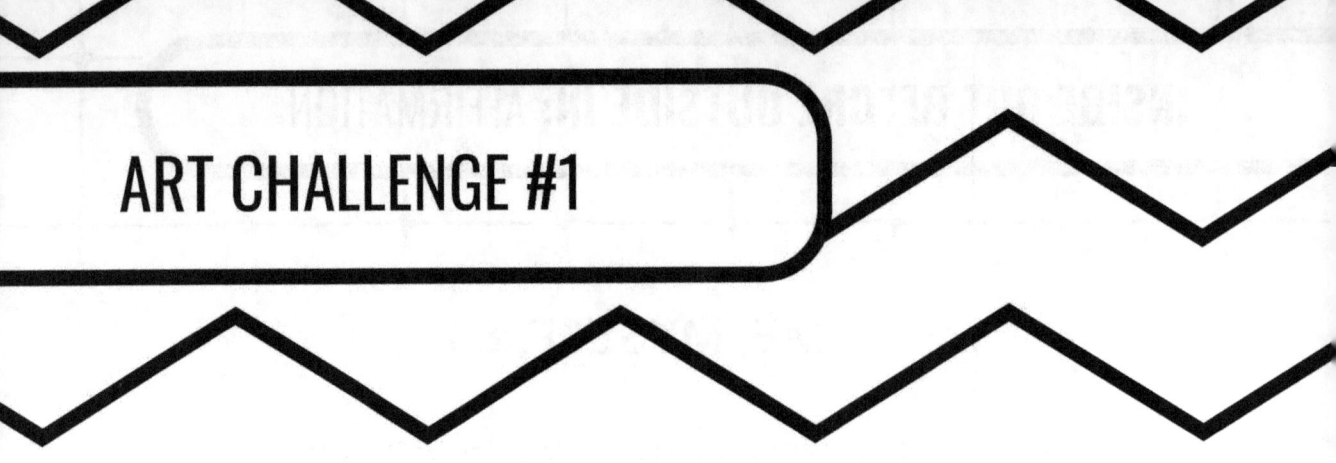

ART CHALLENGE #1

VISUAL ART

Utilize photography, painting, digital media, sketching, sculpture, collage, crafts, etc. to represent the Chosen Life principle through visual art.

CHALLENGE

Declutter your email and social media platforms. Organize your cell phone homescreen.

OCTOBER 1

INSIDE OUT BEFORE OUTSIDE IN

"Success comes from the inside out. In order to change what is on the outside, you must first change what is on the inside."
— *Idowu Koyenikan.*

What does it mean to be successful? Where are you in this journey? Does your definition include more of the internal or external factors? Explain.

_____
_____
_____
_____
_____
_____
_____
_____
_____
_____
_____

Proverbs 16:3 "Commit your work to the Lord, and your plans will be established." ESV

OCTOBER 2

INSIDE OUT BEFORE OUTSIDE IN

"It's okay to not be okay all the time." — Minter Dial.

What does it mean to be okay? What does it look-feel-sound like? How do you move from being not okay towards okay and great? Explain.

_____
_____
_____
_____
_____
_____
_____
_____
_____
_____

Romans 7:24 "Wretched (person) that I am! Who will deliver me from this body of death? Thanks be to God through Jesus Christ our Lord!" ESV

INSIDE OUT BEFORE OUTSIDE IN

"Our life will be more serene and beautiful when we start living from the inside out." — Bhuwan Thapaliya

What does a serene life look like for you? Paint the picture by describing the top 3-6 ingredients. Why are these components important and/or why not?

_____
_____
_____
_____
_____
_____
_____
_____
_____
_____
_____
_____
_____
_____

Psalm 37:4 "Delight yourself in the Lord, and He will give you the desires of your heart." ESV

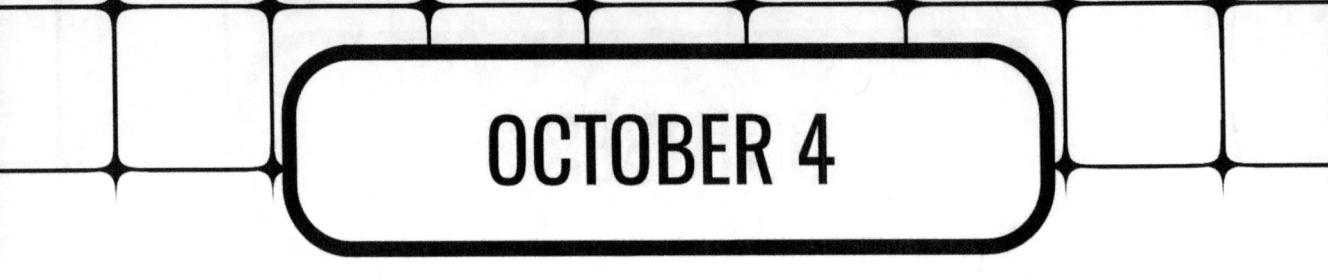

INSIDE OUT BEFORE OUTSIDE IN

"The leader who is able to embrace his or her imperfections is the one who will most likely inspire sustainable and healthy success."
— *Minter Dial*

As a leader, would you use your imperfections to inspire? Do you embrace your imperfections? Why or why not? How could this help or hurt?

_____
_____
_____
_____
_____
_____
_____
_____
_____
_____

John 3:30 "He must increase, but I must decrease." ESV

OCTOBER 5

INSIDE OUT BEFORE OUTSIDE IN

"True happiness starts in the core of our true selves as a constant, a guidepost, a default, and a strength that shines from the inside out." — Elaina Marie

Are you truly happy? Why or why not? Does your happiness showcase to others from the inside out?

_____
_____
_____
_____
_____
_____
_____
_____
_____
_____
_____
_____

1 Kings 2:3 "And keep the charge of the Lord your God, walking in His ways and keeping His statutes, His commandments, His rules, and His testimonies… that you may prosper in all that you do and wherever you turn." ESV

OCTOBER 6

INSIDE OUT BEFORE OUTSIDE IN

"Be who you are and say what you feel because those who mind don't matter and those who matter don't mind."–Dr. Seuss

How does it feel to be your most authentic self and to say what you feel? Why does it matter? How does it impact your relationships and interactions? Explain.

_____
_____
_____
_____
_____
_____
_____
_____
_____
_____
_____

1 Corinthians 15:10 "But by the grace of God I am what I am, and His grace to me was not without effect." ESV

OCTOBER 7

INSIDE OUT BEFORE OUTSIDE IN

"Those who know how to make connections, to connect the dots, ideas and people will be those who know how to surf on the wave of change that is ahead." — Minter Dial

How effective are you with making connections and recognizing patterns? How may connecting people and ideas keep you on the path of innovation and the direction of the culture? How will this type of insight help you to embrace change?

_____
_____
_____
_____
_____
_____
_____
_____
_____
_____

Ephesians 4:22-24 "Put off your old self, which belongs to your former manner of life and is corrupt through deceitful desires, and be renewed in the spirit of your minds, and put on the new self, created after the likeness of God in true righteousness and holiness." ESV

ART CHALLENGE #2

WORD ART

Utilize acrostic poetry, short stories, word cloud, etc. to represent the Chosen Life principle through word art.

CHALLENGE

Write down 10 things that you love about yourself. Focus on your character and internal attributes.

ART CHALLENGE #3

MOVEMENT ART

Utilize dance, human twister poses, acting, etc. to represent the Chosen Life principle through movement art.

CHALLENGE

Play music that you like and express your creativity through movement art.

OCTOBER 8

INSIDE OUT BEFORE OUTSIDE IN

"When you live from the inside out, it doesn't matter how chaotic the world around you is. You're at peace with yourself and walk with your own pace." — Assegid Habtewold

When was the last time you embodied peace when everything around you was chaotic? How did you make it happen? What does it mean to be at peace with yourself inside out? Explain.

_____

Proverbs 3:5-6 "Trust in the Lord with all your heart, and do not lean on your own understanding. In all your ways acknowledge Him, and He will make straight your paths." ESV

OCTOBER 9

INSIDE OUT BEFORE OUTSIDE IN

"To be fair, I spend most days living inside my head—hoping that when I finally open my mouth or put pen to paper, what comes out will matter." - Author: Ryan J. Pemberton

Are you a deep thinker or an over-thinker? How does this help or hurt you? How does what you think, say, and write matter? Are you destined to share it with the world? Explain.

_____
_____
_____
_____
_____
_____
_____
_____
_____
_____

Matthew 15:10-11 "Hear and understand: it is not what goes into the mouth that defiles a person, but what comes out of the mouth; this defiles a person." ESV

OCTOBER 10

INSIDE OUT BEFORE OUTSIDE IN

"No amount of outside achievement fixes inside hurts."
—Lysa TerKeurst

How do outside achievements fulfill you?
Do they heal your past wounds or traumas?
Why do people spend so much time on success if it doesn't guarantee success?

___

Mark 8:36 "For what does it profit a man to gain the whole world and forfeit his soul?" ESV

OCTOBER 11

INSIDE OUT BEFORE OUTSIDE IN

"Life is tough. You need to be tougher or it will turn you inside out." —Kristin Hannah

How are you navigating your life? Is it easy, smooth, or tough? Do you rely on internal or the external factors to make the process seamless? How does this help or hurt?

_____
_____
_____
_____
_____
_____
_____
_____
_____
_____

Matthew 16:24 Then Jesus told his disciples, "If anyone would come after me, let him deny himself and take up his cross and follow me." ESV

OCTOBER 12

INSIDE OUT BEFORE OUTSIDE IN

"If you want to get rich on the outside, then become rich on the inside first. You will reap on the outside what you sow on the inside." — Jeanette Coron

How does one become rich on the inside? Is becoming rich in the mind the prerequisite to becoming rich on the outside? Why or why not? Explain.

_____
_____
_____
_____
_____
_____
_____
_____
_____
_____
_____

Matthew 6:20-21 "But store up for yourselves treasures in heaven, where moths and vermin do not destroy, and where thieves do not break in and steal. For where your treasure is, there your heart will be also." ESV

OCTOBER 13

INSIDE OUT BEFORE OUTSIDE IN

"Work hard in silence, let your success be your noise."
— Anonymous

What does it mean to work hard? What obstacles develop on the road to success? Which ones cause you to sound your voice and advocate? Should success be a silent celebration?

_____
_____
_____
_____
_____
_____
_____
_____
_____
_____
_____
_____

2 Thessalonians 3:10-12 "If anyone is not willing to work, let him not eat. For we hear that some among you walk in idleness, not busy at work, but busybodies. Now such persons we command and encourage in the Lord Jesus Christ to do their work quietly and to earn their own living." ESV

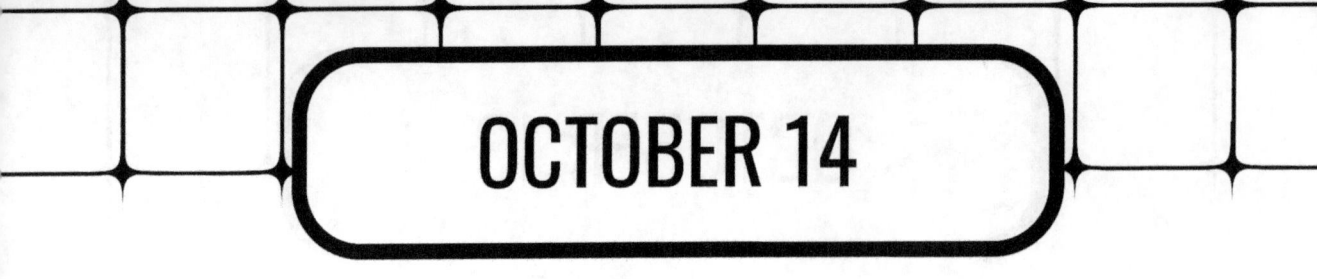

INSIDE OUT BEFORE OUTSIDE IN

"Life begins at the end of your comfort zone."
— Neale Donald Walsch

Do you live within the perimeters of comfort? Why or why not? Do you take risks? What would happen if you pushed past your zone of comfort into the zone of fearlessness?

___

1 Corinthians 15:58 "Therefore, my beloved (believers) be steadfast, immovable, always abounding in the work of the Lord, knowing that in the Lord your labor is not in vain." ESV

OCTOBER 15

INSIDE OUT BEFORE OUTSIDE IN

"Two things define you: Your patience when you have nothing and your attitude when you have everything." – Imam Ali

Patience is expensive, how much have you paid in patience? Are you patient when you have nothing? What is your attitude when you become successful? Is attitude and patience the recipe of success?

_____
_____
_____
_____
_____
_____
_____
_____
_____
_____

Proverbs 10:4 "A slack hand causes poverty, but the hand of the diligent makes rich." ESV

ART CHALLENGE #4

MUSIC ART

Utilize instrumentals, lyrics, or diverse genres to represent the Chosen Life principle through music art.

CHALLENGE

Think of a song or genre that speaks to your most organic inner being.

ART CHALLENGE #5

CULINARY ART

Utilize cooking, baking, drink design, and the 5 senses (sight, touch, smell, taste, and hearing) to represent the Chosen Life principle through culinary art.

CHALLENGE

Indulge in a dessert from your childhood or share a story about it to someone close.

OCTOBER 16

INSIDE OUT BEFORE OUTSIDE IN

"If you want something you have never had, you must be willing to do something you have never done." – Thomas Jefferson

What are you willing to do differently to become your best self? What do you want that you never had? Why? Is the sacrifice worth the pay off? Explain.

_____
_____
_____
_____
_____
_____
_____
_____
_____
_____
_____

Mark 2:22 "No one puts new wine into old wineskins. If he does, the wine will burst the skins—and the wine is destroyed, and so are the skins. But new wine is for fresh wineskins." ESV

OCTOBER 17

INSIDE OUT BEFORE OUTSIDE IN

"The greatest pleasure in life is doing what people say you cannot do." – Walter Bagehot

Is it better to exceed people's expectations or your own? When was the last time you accomplished something that others said you couldn't? How did it feel and why does it matter? Explain.

_____
_____
_____
_____
_____
_____
_____
_____
_____
_____
_____
_____
_____

Philippians 4:13 "I can do all things through Christ who strengthens me." ESV

INSIDE OUT BEFORE OUTSIDE IN

"An entire sea of water can't sink a ship unless it gets inside the ship. Similarly, the negativity of the world can't put you down unless you allow it to get inside you." — Goi Nasu

How challenging is it to keep the negativity of the world away from your thoughts, family, career, etc.,? Who do you attract, optimists, pessimists, realists, or idealist? How do they add value or devalue your life experiences?

_____
_____
_____
_____
_____
_____
_____
_____
_____
_____

John 17:14 "I have given them your word, and the world has hated them because they are not of the world, just as I am not of the world." ESV

OCTOBER 19

INSIDE OUT BEFORE OUTSIDE IN

"The world is changed by your example, not by your opinion."
— Paulo Coelho

Which has more value, your opinion or your example? Which requires more of your time, energy, and effort? How may you use your example to change the arenas that you influence (i.e., job, family members, etc.)?

_____
_____
_____
_____
_____
_____
_____
_____
_____
_____

Titus 2:7-8 "Show yourself in all respects to be a model of good works, and in your teaching show integrity, dignity, and sound speech that cannot be condemned, so that an opponent may be put to shame, having nothing evil to say about us." ESV

OCTOBER 20

INSIDE OUT BEFORE OUTSIDE IN

"Worry a little bit every day and in a lifetime you will lose a couple of years. If something is wrong, fix it if you can. But train yourself not to worry: Worry never fixes anything."
— Ernest Hemingway

How much time do you spend worrying? Would you stop if it was guaranteed to subtract hours, days, or years off of your life on the back end? What strategies would you use to decrease your worry behavior? What would you do to redirect your thinking to focus on solutions that fix the problem?

_____
_____
_____
_____
_____
_____
_____
_____

Matthew 6:27 "And which of you by worrying can add a single hour to your span of life?" ESV

OCTOBER 21

INSIDE OUT BEFORE OUTSIDE IN

"It's not the load that breaks you down, it's the way you carry it."
— Lou Holtz

How do you process your bad stress?
What is your coping mechanism? Is it positive or negative?

_____
_____
_____
_____
_____
_____
_____
_____
_____
_____
_____

2 Corinthians 12:9 "But He said to me, "My grace is sufficient for you, for my power is made perfect in weaknesses, so that the power of Christ may rest upon me." ESV

OCTOBER 22

INSIDE OUT BEFORE OUTSIDE IN

"Life is from the inside out. When you shift on the inside, life shifts on the outside." - Kamal Ravikant

Do you want to grow and self-improve? Do you desire to change for the better?
What internal work are you willing to do?
Is it more difficult to change on the inside or the outside? Why or why not?

_____

_____

_____

_____

_____

_____

_____

_____

_____

Proverbs 21:21 "Whoever pursues righteousness and kindness will find life, righteousness, and honor." ESV

OCTOBER 23

INSIDE OUT BEFORE OUTSIDE IN

"There is a difference between giving up and knowing when you have enough" – Unknown

Do you know when you will have enough? When will enough be enough? What does that look-feel-sound like according to your expectations?

_____
_____
_____
_____
_____
_____
_____
_____
_____
_____
_____
_____

Romans 12:11-12 "Do not be slothful in zeal, be fervent in spirit, serve the Lord. Rejoice in hope, be patient in tribulation, be constant in prayer." ESV

ART CHALLENGE #6

FASHION ART

Utilize clothing, make-up, or jewelry art, interior design work, etc. to represent the Chosen Life principle through fashion art.

CHALLENGE

Photo travel for an epic fashion moment of the past and take a current photo to create a side-by-side look.

ART CHALLENGE #7

SILENT ART

Utilize meditation, mindfulness, and quiet time, etc. to represent the Chosen Life principle through silent art.

CHALLENGE

Unplug for at least 2 hours.

INSIDE OUT BEFORE OUTSIDE IN

"Life is a question and how we live it is our answer."
–Gary Keller

What question does your life pose/ask? Why? What is the answer to that question as represented by the way you live your life?

_____
_____
_____
_____
_____
_____
_____
_____
_____
_____
_____
_____

Ephesians 5:15-16 "Look carefully then how you walk, not as unwise but as wise, making the best use of the time, because the days are evil." ESV

OCTOBER 25

INSIDE OUT BEFORE OUTSIDE IN

"A healthy outside starts from the inside." –Robert Urich

Are you living a healthy life? What is your definition of healthy? What does it look-feel-sound like inside out?

_____
_____
_____
_____
_____
_____
_____
_____
_____
_____
_____
_____
_____
_____

1 Corinthians 6:19 "Do you not know that your body is a temple of the Holy Spirit within you, whom you have from God? You are not your own." ESV

OCTOBER 26

INSIDE OUT BEFORE OUTSIDE IN

"In the midst of movement and chaos, keep stillness inside of you." –Deepak Chopra

How do you stay still in the midst of chaos?
Does that stillness begin on the inside or outside? Why or why not?

_____
_____
_____
_____
_____
_____
_____
_____
_____
_____
_____
_____
_____

Psalm 46:10 "Be still, and know that I am God." ESV

OCTOBER 27

INSIDE OUT BEFORE OUTSIDE IN

"People often say that 'beauty is in the eye of the beholder,' and I say that the most liberating thing about beauty is realizing that you are the beholder. This empowers us to find beauty in places where others have not dared to look, including inside ourselves."
—Salma Hayek

What are 3-5 of the most beautiful qualities about you? When did you first observe them? How have they served you in life? In ways, if any, have you taken them for granted?

_____
_____
_____
_____
_____
_____
_____
_____
_____
_____

Song of Solomon 4:7 "You are altogether beautiful, my love; there is no flaw in you." ESV

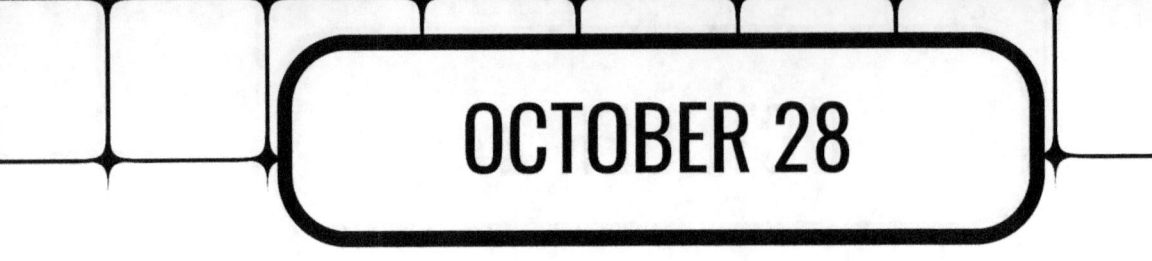

INSIDE OUT BEFORE OUTSIDE IN

"The tragedy of life is what dies inside a man while he lives."
–Albert Schweitzer

What is something that you have allowed to die on the inside? How much has this cost you and others who love you? What needs to happen in order to revive the thing that died (i.e. dream, hope, love, etc.,)?

_____
_____
_____
_____
_____
_____
_____
_____
_____
_____

Galatians 2:20 "I have been crucified with Christ. It is no longer I who live, but Christ who lives in me. And the life I now live in the flesh I live by faith in the Son of God, who loved me and gave Himself for me." ESV

OCTOBER 29

INSIDE OUT BEFORE OUTSIDE IN

"To wear your heart on your sleeve isn't a very good plan; you should wear it inside, where it functions best."
–Margaret Thatcher

Do you wear your heart on your sleeve? Why or why not? How has this helped or hurt you?

_____
_____
_____
_____
_____
_____
_____
_____
_____
_____
_____
_____

Proverbs 4:23 "Keep your heart with all vigilance, for from it flow the springs of life." ESV

OCTOBER 30

INSIDE OUT BEFORE OUTSIDE IN

"Happiness is an inside job."
—William Arthur Ward

Who is responsible for your happiness?
Do you expect your marriage to make you happy? Friendships or Career? What is your personal definition? How do you manage, monitor, and sustain it?

_____
_____
_____
_____
_____
_____
_____
_____
_____
_____
_____
_____

Philippians 4:4 "Rejoice in the Lord always; again I will say, rejoice." ESV

OCTOBER 31

INSIDE OUT BEFORE OUTSIDE IN

"Find a place inside where there's joy, and the joy will burn out the pain." –Joseph Campbell

Can joy burn out pain? Does pain make you appreciate joy? Where does your joy come from?

_____
_____
_____
_____
_____
_____
_____
_____
_____
_____
_____

Ecclesiastes 7:14 "In the day of prosperity be joyful, and in the day of adversity consider: God has made the one as well as the other." ESV

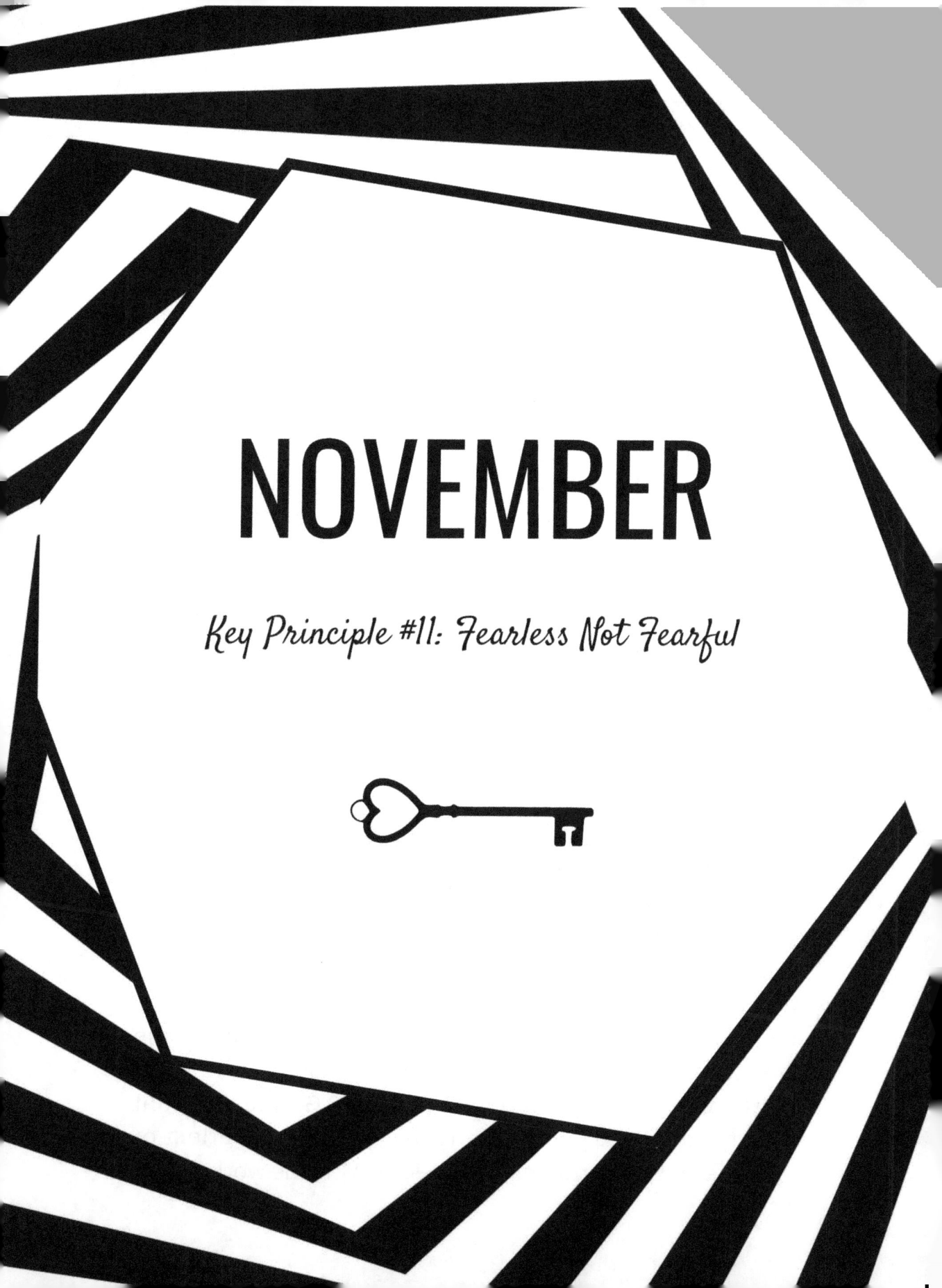

IS FEAR OVERRATED?

FEARLESS NOT FEARFUL

There are several popular misconceptions about courage. In fact, the compartmentalization of the term has become so pervasive that it taints the true brilliance of the word. First off, courage is NOT the absence of fear. It is the willingness to persist or proceed despite the presence of fear. In a lot of ways, courage and fear actually need one another. They make an odd couple, but they tend to bring out the best in each other, and the person in which they occupy.

Second, one of the biggest illusions is the appearance of courage. What does it look like when it shows up? The portrait is often painted with tones of steely eyes, broad shoulders, straight backs, and loud voices.
However, courage can sometimes come in the form of a soft voice with multiple questions. Its hands may be sweaty or shaking. Courage's eyes can sometimes shift to search for the words it wants to say.

It may not always announce itself, but when opportunities to be courageous tap us on the shoulder, how will we respond? Will we give way to fear due to our reluctance to see ourselves through courage's eyes? What internal voices will we entertain and honor? The quest to becoming fearless is in its name: Less Fear. More Courage. Less Doubt. More Belief. Less focus on what we are not. More trust in who we are and what we are becoming. You want to know what courage looks, feels and sounds like? Go stand in front of a mirror. Close your eyes. Take a moment to reflect on your life-path. Now open your eyes. THAT is the work of courage.

FEARLESS NOT FEARFUL: AFFIRMATION

ME, MYSELF, & I

I will receive in this life what I have the courage to ask for and pursue. I recognize that fear means false evidence/events/emotions appearing real. I acknowledge those factors, but refuse to allow them to hinder us in our journey. The evidence of my resilience will manifest to enhance optimism and production.

WE

We receive in this life what we have the courage to ask for and pursue. We recognize that fear means false evidence/events/emotions appearing real. We acknowledge those factors, but refuse to allow them to hinder us in our journey. The evidence of our resilience will manifest in increased optimism and production.

ART CHALLENGE #1

VISUAL ART

Utilize photography, painting, digital media, sketching, sculpture, collage, crafts, etc. to represent the Chosen Life principle through visual art.

CHALLENGE

Compliment yourself when you stand in the mirror naked.

NOVEMBER 1

FEARLESS NOT FEARFUL

"Fear doesn't exist anywhere except in the mind."
— Dale Carnegie

Is fear...a war that is waged against the mind or the reality of actual threats? Why or why not?

_____
_____
_____
_____
_____
_____
_____
_____
_____
_____
_____
_____
_____

Psalm 34:4 "I sought the Lord, and He answered me and delivered me from all my fears." ESV

NOVEMBER 2

FEARLESS NOT FEARFUL

"A river cuts through rock, not because of its power, but because of its persistence." — Jim Watkins

What does it mean to be fearless? Who is the most fearless, a person who is powerful or a person who is persistent? Explain.

_____
_____
_____
_____
_____
_____
_____
_____
_____
_____
_____
_____
_____
_____

1 Corinthians 15:58 "Therefore...be steadfast, immovable, always abounding in the work of the Lord, knowing that in the Lord your labor is not in vain." ESV

NOVEMBER 3

FEARLESS NOT FEARFUL

"Let us not pray to be sheltered from dangers but to be fearless when facing them." –Rabindranath Tagore

Is it possible to avoid or hide from danger? Does a fearless person pray? Does a fearless person fight, flight, or freeze?
What does it look like to face your fears? Explain.

_____
_____
_____
_____
_____
_____
_____
_____
_____
_____

Isaiah 41:10 "Fear not, for I am with you; be not dismayed, for I am your God; I will strengthen you, I will help you, I will uphold you with my righteous right hand." ESV

NOVEMBER 4

FEARLESS NOT FEARFUL

"Beneath every excuse lies a fear. Practice being fearless."
— Robin Sharma

What are the last 3 excuses you used to prevent you from moving forward? What is the root cause? Explain. Is there a pattern of fear? Is there a family member who reminds you of these patterns? Explain.

_____
_____
_____
_____
_____
_____
_____
_____
_____
_____
_____
_____

2 Timothy 1:7 "For God gave us a spirit not of fear but of power and love and self-control." ESV

NOVEMBER 5

FEARLESS NOT FEARFUL

"When you explore your fears, then you set yourself free."
— Stephen Richards

What is the definition of freedom?
Is the exploration of fear the recipe for freeing yourself?

___

Deuteronomy 31:6 "Be strong and courageous. Do not fear or be in dread of them, for it is the Lord your God who goes with you. He will not leave you or forsake you." ESV

NOVEMBER 6

FEARLESS NOT FEARFUL

"Everything you've ever wanted is sitting on the other side of fear." – George Addair

Make a list of at least 3-6 things that bring you fear. What patterns do you notice? Is there a such thing as good fear? Explain.

_____
_____
_____
_____
_____
_____
_____
_____
_____
_____
_____
_____

Joshua 1:9 "Have I not commanded you? Be strong and courageous. Do not be frightened, and do not be dismayed, for the Lord your God is with you wherever you go." ESV

NOVEMBER 7

FEARLESS NOT FEARFUL

"I don't think you should wait. I think you should speak now."
— Taylor Swift

What is the reward in speaking your truth? Is being silent worth the risk of betraying your truth? Why or why not?

_____
_____
_____
_____
_____
_____
_____
_____
_____
_____
_____
_____

Ephesians 4:29 "Let no corrupting talk come out of your mouths, but only such as is good for building up, as fits the occasion, that it may give grace to those who hear." ESV

ART CHALLENGE #2

WORD ART

Utilize acrostic poetry, short stories, word cloud, etc. to represent the Chosen Life principle through word art.

CHALLENGE

Do something positive that makes you happy that you have always wanted to do. Be a risk-taker.

ART CHALLENGE #3

MOVEMENT ART

Utilize dance, human twister poses, acting, etc. to represent the Chosen Life principle through movement art.

CHALLENGE

Dance and move 3 specific body parts in a way that you have not done before or in a long time.

NOVEMBER 8

FEARLESS NOT FEARFUL

"To me, fearless is living in spite of those things that scare you to death." – Taylor Swift

What scares you the most and why? How often do you push in towards the very things that you fear? If you had no distractions, how would you shrink the power of fear and increase the presence of your fearlessness?

_____
_____
_____
_____
_____
_____
_____
_____
_____
_____

Proverbs 29:25 "The fear of man lays a snare, but whoever trusts in the Lord is safe." ESV

NOVEMBER 9

FEARLESS NOT FEARFUL

"Do the thing you fear and the death of fear is certain."
– Ralph Waldo Emerson

What is the best way to kill fear? What is your approach? Make a list of the top 3 areas of fear and create a list of ways to crush it. Explain.

_____
_____
_____
_____
_____
_____
_____
_____
_____
_____
_____

Psalm 23:4 "Even though I walk through the valley of the shadow of death, I will fear no evil, for you are with me." ESV

NOVEMBER 10

FEARLESS NOT FEARFUL

"Be exactly who you are. You can fit in any space you see yourself in. Be fearless." — Dawn Richard

Have you ever questioned if you fit in? Why or why not? How can you show up and be your most authentic self when it seems to be unwelcome? What is your strategy to deal with the consequences and rewards? Explain.

_____

_____

_____

_____

_____

_____

_____

_____

_____

_____

1 Peter 5:6-7 "Humble yourselves, therefore, under the mighty hand of God so that at the proper time He may exalt you, casting all your anxieties on Him, because He cares for you." ESV

NOVEMBER 11

FEARLESS NOT FEARFUL

"It takes a fearless, unflinching love and deep humility to accept the universe as it is." — Ann Druyan

What are 2-3 things you wish you could change about the world?
What efforts have you made, if any to address these issues?
Where are you now in your relationship with these challenges?

_____
_____
_____
_____
_____
_____
_____
_____
_____
_____
_____

1 John 4:18 "There is no fear in love, but perfect love casts out fear. For fear has to do with punishment, and whoever fears has not been perfected in love." ESV

NOVEMBER 12

FEARLESS NOT FEARFUL

"Let me not pray to be sheltered from dangers but to be fearless in facing them." – Rabindranath Tagore

Describe a time when you did something while afraid. What was the outcome? What did you learn about yourself?

_____
_____
_____
_____
_____
_____
_____
_____
_____
_____

Psalm 56:3-4 "When I am afraid, I put my trust in you. In God, whose word I praise, in God I trust; I shall not be afraid. What can flesh do to me?" ESV

NOVEMBER 13

FEARLESS NOT FEARFUL

"To escape fear, you have to go through it, not around."
— *Richie Norton*

What does it mean to defeat fear? Do you go around it, crush it, go through it, or escape fear? Which approach is best? Why or why not?

_____
_____
_____
_____
_____
_____
_____
_____
_____
_____
_____
_____

Isaiah 41:13 "For I, the Lord your God, hold your right hand; it is I who say to you, "Fear not, I am the one who helps you." ESV

NOVEMBER 14

FEARLESS NOT FEARFUL

"The power of one, if fearless and focused, is formidable, but the power of many working together is better."
— Gloria Macapagal Arroyo

What does it mean to be fearless? Is fearlessness accomplished in isolation or by working as a team? Why or why not? Explain.

_____
_____
_____
_____
_____
_____
_____
_____
_____
_____

Hebrews 10:24-25 "And let us consider how to stir up one another to love and good works, not neglecting to meet together, as is the habit of some, but encouraging one another, and all the more as you see the Day drawing near." ESV

NOVEMBER 15

FEARLESS NOT FEARFUL

"Be strong, be fearless, be beautiful. And believe that anything is possible when you have the right people there to support you."
— Misty Copeland

Does fearlessness require support from others? Does fearlessness become more possible with the right people and less possible with the wrong people? Do the people you permit to exist in your space encourage and empower you to be strong, powerful, and fearless? Explain.

_____

_____

_____

_____

_____

_____

_____

_____

_____

_____

Deuteronomy 3:22 "You shall not fear them, for it is the Lord your God who fights for you." ESV

ART CHALLENGE #4

MUSIC ART

Utilize instrumentals, lyrics, or diverse genres to represent the Chosen Life principle through music art.

CHALLENGE

Think of a song or a music genre that puts you in "fearless" mode.

ART CHALLENGE #5

CULINARY ART

Utilize cooking, baking, drink design, and the 5 senses (sight, touch, smell, taste, and hearing) to represent the Chosen Life principle through culinary art.

CHALLENGE

Bake a breakfast, lunch, or dinner item from a different culture or genre.

NOVEMBER 16

FEARLESS NOT FEARFUL

"Watch a child play, and you will see real power. They are fearless." – Gray Scott

When was the last time you watched young children play? What are the characteristics of fearlessness as described through child's play? What lessons can adults learn?

_____
_____
_____
_____
_____
_____
_____
_____
_____
_____
_____

Matthew 18:3 "Truly, I say to you, unless you turn and become like children, you will never enter the kingdom of heaven." ESV

NOVEMBER 17

FEARLESS NOT FEARFUL

"Teenagers are a great audience and they are fearless about asking what they want to know." – Sarah Dessen

Do you ask questions like a fearless teenager?
Are you a great audience for the things that you want to know? Explain.

_____
_____
_____
_____
_____
_____
_____
_____
_____
_____
_____

Matthew 21:15-16 And Jesus said to them, "Yes; have you never read, Out of the mouth of infants and nursing babies you have prepared praise'?" ESV

NOVEMBER 18

FEARLESS NOT FEARFUL

"I don't always feel fierce and fearless, but I do feel like I'm a rock star at being human." — Tracee Ellis Ross

Are you a rock star at being human? Do you overcompensate through actions and deeds? Explain. When have you felt fierce and fearless? Why or why not?

_____
_____
_____
_____
_____
_____
_____
_____
_____
_____

Mark 5:36 "Do not fear, only believe." ESV

NOVEMBER 19

FEARLESS NOT FEARFUL

"I used to be really afraid and anxious of taking on too much, and the older I'm getting, the more fearless I'm becoming. Life is so much more relaxed when you're like that." – Alesha Dixon

Is fearlessness a recipe to be more relaxed? Does it cure being afraid and anxious? Can fearlessness co-exist with fear and anxiety? Explain.

_____
_____
_____
_____
_____
_____
_____
_____
_____
_____

Psalm 27:1 "The Lord is my light and my salvation; whom shall I fear? The Lord is the stronghold of my life; of whom shall I be afraid?" ESV

NOVEMBER 20

FEARLESS NOT FEARFUL

"The older people get... they seem to become fearless. They go right out into the world. It's astounding. Maybe they can't see or they can't hear, but they walk out into the street and take life as it comes. They're models of courage, in a strange way."
– James Hillman

Are you becoming more fearful or fearless the older you become? Are you taking life as it comes? Is your life experience positive or negative? Who do you admire and how does their courage inspire you?

_____
_____
_____
_____
_____
_____
_____
_____
_____

1 Peter 5:2 "Shepherd the flock of God that is among you, exercising oversight, not under compulsion, but willingly, as God would have you; not for shameful gain, but eagerly." ESV

NOVEMBER 21

FEARLESS NOT FEARFUL

"Do not fear mistakes. You will know failure. Continue to reach out." – Benjamin Franklin

How do you view your mistakes? Are they a natural part of the growth process or a sign of failure? Are they a stepping stone or a ditch? Why or why not? Explain.

_____
_____
_____
_____
_____
_____
_____
_____
_____
_____

John 14:1 "Let not your heart be troubled. Neither let it be afraid." ESV

NOVEMBER 22

FEARLESS NOT FEARFUL

"Being fearless of failure arms you to break the rules. In doing so, you may change the culture and just possibly, for a moment, change life itself." – Malcolm McLaren

Are you a rule breaker? Why or why not? Do you attribute this characteristic to most change agents? Is risk-taking required to change the culture? Explain.

_____

_____

_____

_____

_____

_____

_____

_____

_____

_____

1 Chronicles 28:20 "Be strong and courageous and do it. Do not be afraid and do not be dismayed, for the Lord God, even my God, is with you. He will not leave you or forsake you, until all the work for the service of the house of the Lord is finished." ESV

NOVEMBER 23

FEARLESS NOT FEARFUL

"Inaction breeds doubt and fear. Action breeds confidence and courage. If you want to conquer fear, do not sit home and think about it. Go out and get busy." – Dale Carnegie

What does it mean to have confidence and courage? If fearlessness means taking action, what will you do to move towards action instead of remaining stuck in thought? Explain.

_____
_____
_____
_____
_____
_____
_____
_____
_____
_____

Romans 12:11 "Do not be slothful in zeal, be fervent in spirit, serve the Lord." ESV

ART CHALLENGE #6

FASHION ART

Utilize clothing, make-up, or jewelry art, interior design work, etc. to represent the Chosen Life principle through fashion art.

CHALLENGE

Go shopping with a friend and give them permission to show you an outfit, hat, jewelry, or makeup samples that they think you would look fantastic wearing.

ART CHALLENGE #7

SILENT ART

Utilize meditation, mindfulness, and quiet time, etc. to represent the Chosen Life principle through silent art.

CHALLENGE

Meditate on a current obstacle or challenge. Visualize overcoming it and the fear that surrounds it.

NOVEMBER 24

FEARLESS NOT FEARFUL

"It is not the critic who counts; not the man who points out how the strong man stumbles, or where the doer of deeds could have done them better. The credit belongs to the man who is actually in the arena, whose face is marred by dust and sweat and blood; who strives valiantly; who errs, who comes short again and again... who at the best knows in the end the triumph of high achievement, and who at the worst, if he fails, at least fails while daring greatly." — Teddy Roosevelt

How do you deal with criticism? What are the intrusive thoughts and voices you hear during moments of criticism?
How have you responded to these voices over the course of your life?

_____
_____
_____
_____
_____
_____
_____

Galatians 6:4-5 "But let each one test their own work, and then the reason to boast will be in them alone and not in their neighbor. For each will have to bear their own load." ESV

NOVEMBER 25

FEARLESS NOT FEARFUL

"Boldness doesn't mean rude, obnoxious, loud, or disrespectful. Being bold is being firm, sure, confident, fearless, daring, strong, resilient, and not easily intimidated. It means you're willing to go where you've never been, willing to try what you've never tried, and willing to trust what you've never trusted. Boldness is quiet, not noisy." –Mike Yaconelli

Is there a difference between boldness and arrogance? If so, what is it? What is your perspective on boldness? What role does boldness play in your life?

_____
_____
_____
_____
_____
_____
_____
_____
_____
_____

2 Corinthians 3:12 "Since we have such a hope, we are very bold." ESV

NOVEMBER 26

FEARLESS NOT FEARFUL

"I am totally fearless! Well, of course, I'm not totally fearless. I worry constantly and obsess over things, but I just don't let fear stand in the way of doing something that I really want to do."
—Tom Ford

Name something that fear has prevented you from accomplishing.
What did you tell yourself in that moment?
How has it impacted your life? What steps have you taken to address it?

_____
_____
_____
_____
_____
_____
_____
_____
_____

Psalm 27:3 "Though an army encamp against me, my heart shall not fear; though war arise against me, yet I will be confident." ESV

NOVEMBER 27

FEARLESS NOT FEARFUL

"The eagle has no fear of adversity. We need to be like the eagle and have a fearless spirit of a conqueror!" –Joyce Meyer

In your opinion, what is the most fearless animal in the world?
What attributes qualify it to be crowned fearless?
What makes this animal stand out? What lessons can you learn from it?

_____
_____
_____
_____
_____
_____
_____
_____
_____
_____
_____
_____

Isaiah 40:31 "But they who wait for the Lord shall renew their strength; they shall mount up with wings like eagles; they shall run and not be weary; they shall walk and not faint." ESV

NOVEMBER 28

FEARLESS NOT FEARFUL

"I think that music opens portals and doorways into unknown sectors that it takes courage to leap into. I always think that there's a potential that we all have, and we can emerge, rise up to this potential, when necessary. We have to be fearless, courageous, and draw upon wisdom that we think we don't have."
—Wayne Shorter

Who is the most courageous, daring musical artist that you know? What works or compositions would you point to as examples? Where do you think this courage comes from? How has their courage in music impacted you?

_____

_____

_____

_____

_____

_____

_____

_____

Psalm 40:3 "He put a new song in my mouth, a song of praise to our God. Many will see and fear, and put their trust in the Lord." ESV

NOVEMBER 29

FEARLESS NOT FEARFUL

"Women have always been courageous... They are always fearless when protecting their children and in the last century they have been fearless in the fight for their rights." –Isabel Allende

Who is a woman that exemplifies bravery? What characteristics can you identify that contribute to your assessment?
How do you reconcile the relationship between her personality and her appearance? Are they contrary or complimentary?

_____
_____
_____
_____
_____
_____
_____
_____
_____
_____
_____

Proverbs 31:30 "Charm is deceitful, and beauty is vain, but a woman who fears the Lord is to be praised." ESV

NOVEMBER 30

FEARLESS NOT FEARFUL

"Only the really young are fearless, have the optimism, the romanticism to take unimaginable risks." –Olivia Wilde

Reflect on a significant risk that you took when you were younger. What would you tell yourself if you could go back to that moment? What would that version of yourself tell you if they could talk to you today?

_____
_____
_____
_____
_____
_____
_____
_____
_____
_____

Isaiah 54:13 "All your children shall be taught by the Lord, and great shall be the peace of your children." ESV

DECEMBER

Key Principle #12: Every Day Counts

LIVE THE BEST ARTFUL LIFE... 365!!!!

EVERY DAY COUNTS

Tick tock tick tock. Time talks when you won't. It shows up... even when you don't. It pays attention and documents everything. It takes count... so you don't miss the little things. ... but what is it saying?

Are you wasting it? Playing or weighing its impact with the many excuses. Our misappropriated time uses are proof that time waits for no one. It is consistent. Each day the seconds, minutes, and hours work hard and give birth to a new day. #Teamwork But we are not satisfied? We keep asking and praying for more. Greedy, we must be careful not to spill time like the perfect cup of coffee or hot tea... and are surprised when we're burned.

In a full day you have 24 hours. Live your best life! Pump up the volume on your favorite song. Dance like nobody's watching. Sing... like no one can hear. Believe the words coming out of your mouth. Become your personal "warrior story and anthem" every day.

Live the life you want today. What are you waiting on? Who are you waiting for? Which excuses are weighing you down? Which thoughts need more? Which need less time? What situations and which relationships need to be divided, multiplied, subtracted, or added in order to help you grow and develop?

LIVE THE BEST ARTFUL LIFE... 365!!!!

EVERY DAY COUNTS

Tick toc tick toc. Time will not wait. Go for it! Go get it! Keep moving ahead. Finance your dream. Lead the task of documenting. Write the story. Open the business. Make it happen. Is tomorrow guaranteed?

Only the seconds, minutes, and hours will be left to sound the alarms. For the bold artful souls, your destiny waits with every thought, word spoken, and action. Are you waiting for the life you want to chose you or will you chose it? A chosen life is to live artfully from the inside out in a fearless way because every day counts.

EVERY DAY COUNTS: AFFIRMATION

ME, MYSELF, & I

I will count my gifts and talents one by one, leaving not an hour, minute, or second to complain. I will celebrate and appreciate my personal growth journey so that every victory-no matter how big or small, will attract more (law of attraction). In the end, I don't want to regret the chances I didn't take, the calling I didn't respond to, the challenges I didn't learn from, and the change I resisted. I will make the most of every day, moment, and opportunity. I choose to build a life that is based upon values, principles, and purpose. I will not break apart the work that I have committed to do.

WE

We will count our gifts and talents one by one, leaving not an hour, minute, or second to complain. We will celebrate and appreciate our marriage journey so that every victory- no matter how big or small, will attract more (law of attraction). In the end, we don't want to regret the chances we didn't take, the calling we didn't respond to, the challenges we didn't learn from, and the change we resisted. We will make the most of every day, moment, and opportunity. We choose to build a life together that is built upon values, principles, and purpose. We will not break apart the work that we have committed to do together.

ART CHALLENGE #1

VISUAL ART

Utilize photography, painting, digital media, sketching, sculpture, collage, crafts, etc. to represent the Chosen Life principle through visual art.

CHALLENGE

Create a photo collage of 10 of your favorite people and images reflecting the benefit of their role in your life.

DECEMBER 1

EVERY DAY COUNTS

"Never give up on a dream just because of the time it will take to accomplish it. The time will pass anyway." — Earl Nightingale

What is a childhood dream(s) that you are still pursuing? How long has it been? What inspires you to continue pursuing it?

_____
_____
_____
_____
_____
_____
_____
_____
_____
_____

Psalm 90:12 "So teach us to number our days that we may get a heart of wisdom." ESV

DECEMBER 2

EVERY DAY COUNTS

"The first step to getting anywhere is deciding you're no longer willing to stay where you are." – Anonymous

What people or things did you let go of to get to where you are now? What people or things do you believe you need to let go of to get where you want to go?

_____
_____
_____
_____
_____
_____
_____
_____
_____
_____

Philippians 3:13-14 "But one thing I do: forgetting what lies behind and straining forward to what lies ahead, I press on toward the goal for the prize of the upward call of God in Christ Jesus." ESV

DECEMBER 3

EVERYDAY COUNTS

"If you are depressed you are living in the past. If you are anxious you are living in the future. If you are at peace you are living in the present." – Lao Tzu

What steps or strategies can you use to help you remain fully present in today?
What issues from your past may make this difficult?
What future concerns might pose a threat?

_____
_____
_____
_____
_____
_____
_____
_____
_____
_____

2 Thessalonians 3:16 "Now may the Lord of peace Himself give you peace at all times in every way. The Lord be with you all." ESV

DECEMBER 4

EVERYDAY COUNTS

"A year from now you may wish you had started today."
— Karen Lamb

What necessary, positive change have you been delaying? How has this delay impacted your life? What have been some excuses you've told yourself about not starting the process?

_____
_____
_____
_____
_____
_____
_____
_____
_____
_____

John 9:4 "We must work the works of Him who sent us while it is day; night is coming, when no one can work." ESV

DECEMBER 5

EVERY DAY COUNTS

"I hated every minute of training, but I said, "Don't quit. Suffer now and live the rest of your life as a champion."
— Muhammad Ali

Reflect on a time when you had to wait for something you really wanted.
How long did you wait? Was the wait difficult?
How did you manage your patience?
When you finally gained what you worked for, was it worth it? Why or why not?

_____

_____

_____

_____

_____

_____

_____

_____

_____

1 Timothy 4:7-8 "Train yourself for godliness; for while bodily training is of some value, godliness is of value in every way, as it holds promise for the present life and also for the life to come." ESV

DECEMBER 6

EVERY DAY COUNTS

"If you don't make the time to work on creating the life you want, you're eventually going to be forced to spend a lot of time dealing with a life you don't want." — Kevin Ngo

On a scale of 1-10, how would you score the quality of your personal life? Your professional life? What factors contribute to your score? What adjustments need to be made to increase the score for both areas?

_____
_____
_____
_____
_____
_____
_____
_____
_____
_____
_____

Ecclesiastes 3:11 "He has made everything beautiful in its time." ESV

DECEMBER 7

EVERY DAY COUNTS

"When you want to succeed as bad as you want to breathe, then you'll be successful." — Eric Thomas

What is your definition of success?
How does this definition look, feel, and sound in your everyday life?

_____
_____
_____
_____
_____
_____
_____
_____
_____
_____

Psalm 90:17 "Let the favor of the Lord our God be upon us, and establish the work of our hands upon us; yes, establish the work of our hands!" ESV

ART CHALLENGE #2

WORD ART

Utilize acrostic poetry, short stories, word cloud, etc. to represent the Chosen Life principle through word art.

CHALLENGE

Write 3 beliefs and release 1 limiting belief.

ART CHALLENGE #3

MOVEMENT ART

Utilize dance, human twister poses, acting, etc. to represent the Chosen Life principle through movement art.

CHALLENGE

Practice yoga or do some light stretching. Find 4 poses that make your body come alive.

DECEMBER 8

EVERYDAY COUNTS

"Today I will do what others won't so tomorrow I can do what others can't." – Jerry Rice

What keeps you motivated to diligently pursue success?
What sacrifices have you made in your efforts?
Do you have a belief system or core values that support your process?
If so, what does it consist of?

_____
_____
_____
_____
_____
_____
_____
_____
_____
_____

Psalm 1:1-3 "Blessed is the one who walks not in the counsel of the wicked, nor stands in the way of sinners, nor sits in the seat of scoffers; but their delight is in the law of the Lord, and on His law they meditate day and night. They are like a tree planted by streams of water that yields its fruit in its season, and its leaf does not wither. In all that they do, they prosper." ESV

DECEMBER 9

EVERY DAY COUNTS

"If you don't build your dream someone will hire you to help build theirs." – Tony Gaskins

How have your skills and abilities helped support the goals and dreams of others, both personally and professionally?
How have others supported you in your goals and dreams?
In what ways can you be more intentional in advocating for yourself?

_____
_____
_____
_____
_____
_____
_____
_____
_____
_____

Proverbs 1:10, 18 "My son, if sinners entice you, Do not consent; they lie in wait for their own blood, They lurk secretly for their own lives." ESV

DECEMBER 10

EVERY DAY COUNTS

"I don't count my sit-ups. I only start counting when it starts hurting. When I feel pain, that's when I start counting, because that's when it really counts." – Muhammad Ali

What is your initial thought when you feel pain?
How do you respond to the pain?
How do you respond to what you perceive as the cause (i.e. people, situations, conditions) of your pain? Does it help or harm? Why?

_____
_____
_____
_____
_____
_____
_____
_____
_____
_____

2 Corinthians 4:17 "For this light momentary affliction is preparing for us an eternal weight of glory beyond all comparison." ESV

DECEMBER 11

EVERY DAY COUNTS

"The habits that took years to build, do not take a day to change."
— Susan Powter

How do you exercise patience with yourself during positive and difficult moments? Research suggests that it takes 21 days to break a habit. How long does it take you to break a habit? Why? What is your strategy?

_____
_____
_____
_____
_____
_____
_____
_____
_____
_____

Ephesians 5:1 "Therefore be imitators of God, as beloved children." ESV

DECEMBER 12

EVERY DAY COUNTS

"How we spend our days is, of course, is how we spend our lives." —Annie Dillard

Is how you to spend your days a reflection of how you live your life?
Why or why not?
What are the benefits and what are the potential barriers of this philosophy?

_____
_____
_____
_____
_____
_____
_____
_____
_____
_____

Ephesians 5:16 "Making the best use of the time, because the days are evil." ESV

DECEMBER 13

EVERY DAY COUNTS

"There are only two days in the year that nothing can be done. One is called Yesterday and the other is called Tomorrow. Today is the right day to Love, Believe, Do, and mostly Live."
—Dalai Lama XIV

Are you living for today appropriately?
Are you missing what is occurring or not occurring now because you are distracted by yesterday or tomorrow?
Why or why not?

_____
_____
_____
_____
_____
_____
_____
_____
_____

Matthew 6:34 "Therefore do not worry about tomorrow, for tomorrow will worry about itself. Each day has enough trouble of its own." ESV

DECEMBER 14

EVERY DAY COUNTS

"I'm too busy working on my own grass to notice if yours is greener." – Anonymous

How are you tending to your own grass (i.e. personal goals and dreams)?
Are you regularly distracted by the projects, goals, and work of others?
Why or why not?
How can you begin to ensure that you are focused and fulfilling your purpose?

_____
_____
_____
_____
_____
_____
_____
_____
_____
_____

Galatians 6:4 "But let each one test his own work, and then his reason to boast will be in himself alone and not in his neighbor." ESV

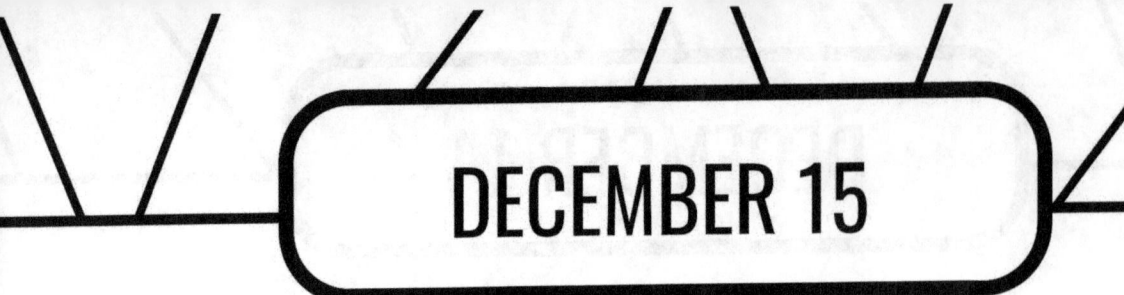

DECEMBER 15

EVERY DAY COUNTS

"Though no one can go back and make a brand new start, anyone can start from now and make a brand new ending." – Carl Bard

How many times have you wished you could have a do-over? Do-overs are very rare. If you focused on today being the fresh start to the rest of your new life, what would you do differently right now? What resources would you need in order to begin this new work and why?

_____
_____
_____
_____
_____
_____
_____
_____
_____
_____

Ezekiel 36:26 "And I will give you a new heart, and a new spirit I will put within you. And I will remove the heart of stone from your flesh and give you a heart of flesh." ESV

ART CHALLENGE #4

MUSIC ART

Utilize instrumentals, lyrics, or diverse genres to represent the Chosen Life principle through music art.

CHALLENGE

Make a playlist of 3 old favorite inspirational songs and 3 new songs you recently discovered. Maybe ask a friend for some new ideas.

ART CHALLENGE #5

CULINARY ART

Utilize cooking, baking, drink design, and the 5 senses (sight, touch, smell, taste, and hearing) to represent the Chosen Life principle through culinary art.

CHALLENGE

Bake a special dessert and share it with others.

DECEMBER 16

EVERY DAY COUNTS

"Be willing to sacrifice what you think you have today for the life that you want tomorrow." – Neil Strauss

Are you willing to sacrifice what you think you have today for the life you want tomorrow? If so, what are the boundaries?
What are you willing and not willing to do? Explain.

_____
_____
_____
_____
_____
_____
_____
_____
_____
_____
_____

Hebrews 13:16 "Do not neglect to do good and to share what you have, for such sacrifices are pleasing to God." ESV

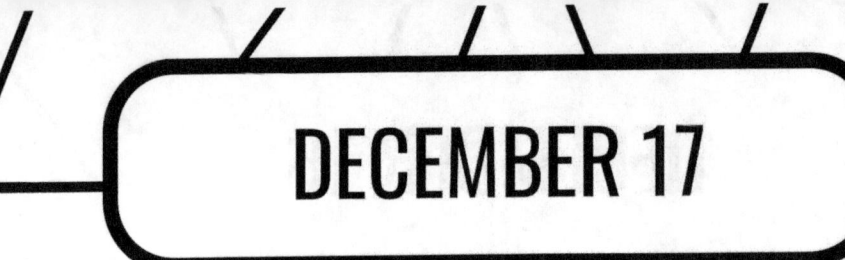

DECEMBER 17

EVERY DAY COUNTS

"Be willing to sacrifice what you think you have today for the life that you want tomorrow." - Neil Strauss

Are you willing to sacrifice what you think you have today for the life you want tomorrow? If so, what are the boundaries?
What are you willing and not willing to do? Explain.

_____
_____
_____
_____
_____
_____
_____
_____
_____
_____

Hebrews 13:16 "Do not neglect to do good and to share what you have, for such sacrifices are pleasing to God." ESV

DECEMBER 18

EVERY DAY COUNTS

"Lean forward into your life. Begin each day as if it were on purpose." – Mary Anne Radmacher

What does it mean to live your life on purpose? How can you make an effort to be a person whose thoughts, words, actions, habits, and character lead to a solid destiny?

_____
_____
_____
_____
_____
_____
_____
_____
_____
_____

Proverbs 16:4 "The Lord has made everything for its purpose, even the wicked for the day of trouble." ESV

DECEMBER 19

EVERY DAY COUNTS

"If you love life, don't waste time, for time is what life is made up of." – Bruce Lee

Do you respect time? What does respecting time look-feel-sound like? Do you require others to respect your time? If so, how?

_____
_____
_____
_____
_____
_____
_____
_____
_____
_____

Psalm 89:47 "Remember how short my time is! For what vanity you have created all the children of man!" ESV

DECEMBER 20

EVERY DAY COUNTS

"Life isn't a matter of milestones, but of moments."
- Rose Kennedy

How do you make the moments in life matter? Do you focus so much on the milestones that the moments get missed?
How can you prevent this from occurring?

_____
_____
_____
_____
_____
_____
_____
_____
_____
_____
_____

Proverbs 21:21 "Whoever pursues righteousness and kindness will find life, righteousness, and honor." ESV

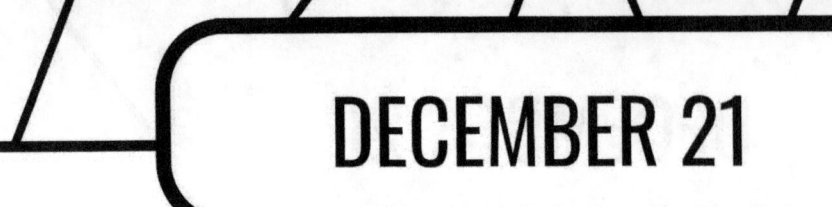

DECEMBER 21

EVERY DAY COUNTS

"Living with intention means saying no to the things that aren't important to us so we can say yes to what matters most."
−Crystal Paine

Are you living with intention? Are you saying no to the things that aren't important so you can say yes to the things that are important? How? Explain.

_____
_____
_____
_____
_____
_____
_____
_____
_____

Matthew 5:37 "Let what you say be simply 'Yes' or 'No'; anything more than this comes from evil." ESV

DECEMBER 22

EVERY DAY COUNTS

"Alright everyone, fresh start. We are going to have a good day, which will turn into a good week, which will turn into a good year, which turns into a good life!" – Joy

What would you do immediately to begin a new habit?
What would the positive reward or impact be today?
In a week? In a year?

_____
_____
_____
_____
_____
_____
_____
_____
_____
_____

Psalm 121:7-8 "The Lord will keep you from all evil; He will keep your life. The Lord will keep your going out and your coming in from this time forth and forevermore." ESV

DECEMBER 23

EVERY DAY COUNTS

"There is no greater agony than bearing an untold story inside you." –Maya Angelou

Do you have an untold story?
Do you bear the agony of a secret?
How can you free yourself?

_____
_____
_____
_____
_____
_____
_____
_____
_____
_____

Psalm 26:7 "Proclaiming thanksgiving aloud, and telling all your wondrous deeds." ESV

ART CHALLENGE #6

FASHION ART

Utilize clothing, make-up, or jewelry art, interior design work, etc. to represent the Chosen Life principle through fashion art.

CHALLENGE

Change the linen on your bed and spray lavender or a calming fragrance on the pillow covers.

ART CHALLENGE #7

SILENT ART

Utilize meditation, mindfulness, and quiet time, etc. to represent the Chosen Life principle through silent art.

CHALLENGE

Follow a guided meditation. Afterwards reflect for 5 minutes in silencce.

DECEMBER 24

EVERY DAY COUNTS

"It's your outlook on life that counts. If you take yourself lightly and don't take yourself too seriously, pretty soon you can find the humor in our everyday lives. And sometimes it can be a lifesaver." –Betty White

What is your outlook on life?
How do you keep your outlook light and not so serious?
How do you find humor in everyday life?
Does this help or hurt? Why or why not?

_____
_____
_____
_____
_____
_____
_____
_____
_____

Psalm 16:11 "You make known to me the path of life; in your presence there is fullness of joy; at your right hand are pleasures forevermore." ESV

DECEMBER 25

EVERY DAY COUNTS

"Art washes away from the soul the dust of everyday life."
—Pablo Picasso

What is the dust (i.e. stressors) of your everyday life? How can art (i.e. creative habits) wash away the dirt and debris of life's issues? Which is the art of your choice? How does it cleanse you?

_____
_____
_____
_____
_____
_____
_____
_____
_____
_____

Exodus 35:35 "He has filled them with skill to do every sort of work..." ESV

DECEMBER 26

EVERY DAY COUNTS

"The remarkable thing is, we have a choice every day regarding the attitude we will embrace for that day." –Charles R. Swindoll

How does your attitude determine your daily mood? What attitude will you embrace when life appears rainy, sunny, cloudy, or windy? Are you satisfied with your attitude of choice?

_____
_____
_____
_____
_____
_____
_____
_____
_____
_____
_____
_____

Philippians 2:14-15 "Do all things without grumbling or disputing, that you may be blameless and innocent, children of God without blemish in the midst of a crooked and twisted generation, among whom you shine as lights in the world…" ESV

DECEMBER 27

EVERY DAY COUNTS

"I am building a fire, and everyday I train, I add more fuel. At just the right moment, I light the match." -Mia Hamm

What are you working towards building?
What is fueling the journey/process?
What are you learning to properly equip you?

_____
_____
_____
_____
_____
_____
_____
_____
_____
_____

Luke 12:49 "I came to cast fire on the earth, and would that it were already kindled!" ESV

DECEMBER 28

EVERY DAY COUNTS

"Gratitude bestows reverence, allowing us to encounter everyday epiphanies, those transcendent moments of awe that change forever how we experience life and the world." –John Milton

How do you practice gratitude?
How does gratitude help you to experience life and to encounter daily epiphanies?

_____
_____
_____
_____
_____
_____
_____
_____
_____
_____
_____

1 Thessalonians 5:18 "Give thanks in all circumstances; for this is the will of God in Christ Jesus for you." ESV

DECEMBER 29

EVERY DAY COUNTS

"Every day holds the possibility of a miracle." –Elizabeth David

Do you believe in miracles? How can you experience one every day?

_____
_____
_____
_____
_____
_____
_____
_____
_____
_____

John 14:12 "Truly, truly, I say to you, whoever believes in me will also do the works that I do; and greater works than these will he do, because I am going to the Father." ESV

DECEMBER 30

EVERY DAY COUNTS

"The problem is when that fun stuff becomes the habit. And I think that's what's happened in our culture. Fast food has become the everyday meal." –Michelle Obama

What habits do you have that are helpful and harmful?
How have the habits become part of your normal everyday process?
How have you allowed quick conveniences to become daily routines?

_____
_____
_____
_____
_____
_____
_____
_____
_____
_____

Ephesians 4:19 "They have become callous and have given themselves up to sensuality, greedy to practice every kind of impurity." ESV

DECEMBER 31

EVERY DAY COUNTS

"You can find poetry in your everyday life, your memory, in what people say on the bus, in the news, or just what's in your heart."
—Carol Ann Duffy

What was the last poetic thing you experienced in the world around you? What was the messaging and what impact did it have on you? Why or why not?

_____
_____
_____
_____
_____
_____
_____
_____
_____
_____

Deuteronomy 32:2 "May my teaching drop as the rain, my speech distill as the dew, like gentle rain upon the tender grass, and like showers upon the herb." ESV

BIBLIOGRAPHY

- English Standard Version Bible. (2001). ESV Online. https://esv.literalword.com/

- English Standard Version Bible, 2001

- Eurich, T. (2017). Why We're Not as Self-Aware as We Think and How Seeing Ourselves Clearly Helps Us Succeed at Work and in Life. Crown Business, New York.

- Wood, K. (2013). The lost art of introspection: Why you must master yourself. Expert Enough. Retrieved from http://expertenough.com/2990/the-lost-art-of-introspection-why-you-must-master-yourself

MEET THE AUTHORS

Who are the authors behind this artful guide to daily living?

CHARMAINE JENNINGS
CMAINE

WALTER JENNINGS
WALLY B

CHARMAINE 'C-MAINE' JENNINGS

Charmaine 'C-Maine' Jennings, is a West Palm Beach native. She is a stellar relationship coach and co-owner of Chosen Life Specialists, LLC. She is a poet, life coach, and artisan of creativity. She is a wife of 20+ years, mother of 2 daughters, advocate, and friend.

She is a veteran educator and began writing poetry as a teenager to deal with depression. She is a national trainer who excels at providing leadership coaching and professional learning opportunities for K-12 principals, coaches, teachers, and interventionists in Florida, Georgia, Indiana, Michigan, Missouri, Ohio, Alabama, Washington D.C., Texas, etc.

Charmaine is a change agent who utilizes arts-integrated strategies, poetry, and artful coaching. Her performances and creative works are typically a call- to-action that encourage personal growth and how to embrace uniqueness in order to overcome trauma and turn obstacles into opportunities.

Learn more at CharmaineCmaineJennings.com.

WALTER 'WALLY B' JENNINGS

Walter "Wally B." Jennings is a native of Tampa, FL. He is a proven innovative instructional coach for business leaders and community stakeholders with 20+ years of experience in creative arts, operational management, and public event coordination. He specializes in pre-marital counseling, officiating wedding ceremonies, marriage intervention, individual life coaching, and youth development.

He is a graduate of Florida A&M University with a Bachelor's Degree in Business Economics. Walter's arts-infused approach have resulted in him earning several national honors and awards as a program director, spoken-word artist, and venue host.

Walter is a husband of 20+ years, proud father of 2 daughters, son, brother, friend, and community leader devoted to exploring life lessons and compelling questions.

For more information, please visit:
WalterWallyBJennings.com or ChosenLifeSpecialists.com

Order Your Copy!
TODAY

Enjoy this non-fairy-tale love story infused with poetry, affirmations, narrations, and bold acts of resilience. Read how this dynamic couple met, fell in love, and encountered many battles. This book is a unique compilation that journeys through the trials and tribulations of long distance dating, college drama, alcoholism, identity crisis, wedding controversies, infidelity, courthouses, relationship trauma, parenting, autism, and more...

Order Your Book Today
HOW THE WEST WAS ONE!

Learn more at: ChosenLifeSpecialists.com!
Learn more at: WalterWallyBJennings.com!
Learn more at: CharmaineCmaineJennings.com!

www.ingramcontent.com/pod-product-compliance
Lightning Source LLC
Chambersburg PA
CBHW060417010526
44118CB00017B/2247